Journey ^{to}the Ring

Behind the Scenes with the 2010 NBA Champion Lakers

TEXT BY

Phil Jackson

PHOTOGRAPHY BY

Andrew D. Bernstein

Journey TO THE Ring

Behind the Scenes with the 2010 NBA Champion Lakers

LOS ANGELES LAKERS

Dedications

To all my relations by blood and by spirit — PJ

To my parents, Len and Beverly. I know you're proud of me as you always were. — ADB

Journey to the Ring: Behind the Scenes with the 2010 NBA Champion Lakers

Copyright © 2010 Phil Jackson.

All photos © 2010 NBA Entertainment. Photos by Andrew D. Bernstein/ NBAE/Getty Images.

The NBA and individual NBA team identifications are used with permission from NBA Properties, Inc. © 2010 NBA Properties, Inc. All rights reserved.

No part of this publication may be stored in a retrieval system, or transmitted in any form by any means, electronic, mechanical, photocopying, or otherwise without the written permission of the publisher, Getty Images, Inc., and NBA Properties, Inc.

ISBN-13: 978-0-9823242-2-6

ISBN-10: 0-9823242-2-7

Library of Congress number: 2010933569

Distributed by BookMasters Distribution Services, Inc. 30 Amberwood Parkway, Ashland, Ohio 44805

Printed and bound in China

First printing September 2010

Editor	Narda Zacchino
Design Director	Tom Trapnell
Photo Editor	Mike Zacchino
Senior Editor	Karen Chaderjian
Copy editor	Johannes Tesselaar
Researcher	Kassandra Zuanich
Proofreader	Barbra Frank
Production Consultant	Richard Willett

Photo of Andrew D. Bernstein on Page 6 by Michael Bernstein

Special thanks to Jeanie Buss, Linda Rambis, and Eugenia Chow of the Lakers; Eric Rachlis, Mike Klein, and Kenwood Yow of Getty Images; Hrishi Karthikeyan of the NBA; and our colleagues at Oceanic Graphic Printing.

Time Capsule Press LLC
P.O. Box 4395
San Leandro, California 94579
www.timecapsulepress.com

TIME CAPSULE PRESS

President and CEO	Dickson Louie
Publisher and Editor	Narda Zacchino

Table of Contents

About the Authors

Phil Jackson, inducted into the Naismith Memorial Basketball Hall of Fame in 2007, has won more NBA titles than any coach. He may prefer the role of "invisible leader," but in any discussion of the NBA's all-time best coach, Jackson's silent advocates are the facts: architect of eleven of the NBA's last twenty champions, holder of the all-time highest winning percentage during the regular season (.705) and playoffs (.697), fastest to 1,000 coaching victories, the only coach to win seventy-two games in a single season and the first coach to win three consecutive titles three times. When winning Game 1 of any playoff series, best-of-five or best-of-seven, Jackson's teams are 48-0.

For all his success, including two rings as a player, Jackson has never fit neatly into one niche. Born in Montana, the son of ministers, an athlete and a coach drawn to the *Way of the Peaceful Warrior*, Jackson takes his players on a journey that covers spaces well beyond basketball. Among his books are *Sacred Hoops*, *The Last Season*, *More Than a Game*, and *Take It All!* Between the Lakers' NBA championships in 2009 and 2010, Jackson wrote the foreword to *Los Angeles Lakers: 50 Amazing Years in the City of Angels*.

Andrew D. Bernstein, the NBA's Senior Director of Photography, has shot every NBA Finals since 1983, covering more championship series games than any photographer. He has a permanent exhibit at the Naismith Memorial Basketball Hall of Fame and his photographs appear in *Sports Illustrated*, *ESPN Magazine*, *Time*, *Newsweek*, and many international publications.

Bernstein graduated from Art Center College of Design in Pasadena, California, and his company, Bernstein Associates, has been official photographer for most of Los Angeles' professional sports teams and venues. Athletes at the highest level say they trust Bernstein to capture personal moments, and they give him high praise: "Andy's one of the guys that created the image of the NBA," says Earvin "Magic" Johnson. Bernstein's photographs appear in his own book, *NBA Hoop Shots: Classic Moments from a Super Era* as well as *America's Dream Team*, *NBA Jam Session*, *NBA at 50*, *Basketball's Best Shots*, and three Lakers' titles, including *Dynasty!!!*

A longtime volunteer and mentor, Bernstein is active on the board of the Heart of Los Angeles (HOLA), an inner city youth center, and Autism Speaks.

Lakers 2009-10 Roster

Player	Position	Height	Weight	DOB	School	Years Pro
Ron Artest	Forward	6-7	260	Nov. 13, 1979	St. John's, 1999	10
Shannon Brown	Guard	6-4	210	Nov. 29, 1985	Michigan State, 2006	3
Kobe Bryant	Guard	6-6	205	Aug. 23, 1978	Lower Merion (PA) HS, 1996	13
Andrew Bynum	Center	7-0	285	Oct. 27, 1987	St. Joseph (NJ) HS, 2005	4
Jordan Farmar	Guard	6-2	180	Nov. 30, 1986	UCLA, 2006	3
Derek Fisher	Guard	6-1	210	Aug. 9, 1974	Arkansas-Little Rock, 1996	13
Pau Gasol	Forward/Center	7-0	250	July 6, 1980	University of Barcelona	8
Didier Ilunga-Mbenga	Center	7-0	255	Dec. 30, 1980	Kinshasa, Dem. Rep. of Congo	5
Adam Morrison	Forward	6-8	205	July 19, 1984	Gonzaga, 2006	2
Lamar Odom	Forward	6-10	230	Nov. 6, 1979	Rhode Island, 2001	10
Josh Powell	Forward/Center	6-9	240	Jan. 25, 1983	North Carolina State, 2005	4
Sasha Vujacic	Guard	6-7	205	March 8, 1984	Ekonomska Sola	5
Luke Walton	Forward	6-8	235	March 28, 1980	Arizona, 2003	6

HEAD COACH
Phil Jackson

ASSISTANT COACHES
Frank Hamblen
Brian Shaw
Jim Cleamons
Chuck Person

ATHLETIC TRAINER
Gary Vitti

ASSISTANT
ATHLETIC TRAINER
Marco Nuñez

DIRECTOR, ATHLETIC
PERFORMANCE/
PLAYER DEVELOPMENT
Robert "Chip" Schaefer

MASSAGE THERAPIST
Marko Yrjovuori

ATHLETIC PERFORMANCE
COORDINATOR
Alex McKechnie

EQUIPMENT MANAGER
Rudy Garciduenas

Top row: Robert "Chip" Schaefer, special assistant coach Kareem Abdul-Jabbar, Frank Hamblen, Phil Jackson, Brian Shaw, Jim Cleamons, special assistant coach Craig Hodges, Alex McKechnie. Middle row: Rudy Garciduenas, Gary Vitti, Derek Fisher, Shannon Brown, Adam Morrison, Kobe Bryant, Sasha Vujacic, Jordan Farmar, Marco Nuñez, Marko Yrjovuori. Bottom row: Luke Walton, Josh Powell, DJ Mbenga, Pau Gasol, owner Jerry Buss, executive vice president of player personnel Jim Buss, Andrew Bynum, Lamar Odom, Ron Artest.

Journey to the Ring

BY PHIL JACKSON

WHEN I WAS a young man, I had a hero in Mickey Mantle. In 1957, a publication devoted an entire issue to Mickey's career through the 1956 MVP season, highlighted with many photographs. As a fan, I looked through that publication until the pages were dog-eared: The fall Mickey had in the outfield six years earlier and the torn knee ligaments that slowed down his early years; with his buddies, Yogi Berra and Billy Martin, at a movie premiere with their wives; and postgame locker room shots where he was celebrating after a heroic game.

These types of photographs have lived in my memory as the images of a great player. This book, *Journey to the Ring*, has the photographs that will help people relive a very memorable NBA season, much as I relived the New York Yankees' 1956 season.

06.08.10 — BOSTON

On a clipboard, I diagram plays, in this case what we would like to do with the first two possessions of the ball in Game 3 of the NBA Finals.

The 2009-10 season was one in which the Los Angeles Lakers were able to redeem a loss to the Boston Celtics from 2008, when Boston rode the white horse all the way to the championship. This year, 2010, we were the favorites from Day One and had to defend our very fickle crown. It was one that will live in the memories of many Los Angeles fans who remember all those Boston series that came up short in the 1960s. This was a seven-game series. This one was ours.

The NBA Finals in 1991 put Andy Bernstein and me together when he was covering that championship series and the Chicago Bulls won their first NBA Finals against the Los Angeles Lakers. For two decades, Andy and I have been dodging each other as he gets his one hundred shots a game and I have to maneuver around his camera. He is a familiar person to the players and gets along with them to the extent they make a space, maybe even pose, for him.

As the season goes on, Andy gets more and more access to our games as the NBA amps up the publicity for the playoffs. So there have been a number of times he has asked for access on our team plane and some shots from the plane and team buses going to games.

In 2009, after our NBA championship win over the Orlando Magic, Andy asked me whether I would consider writing the narrative for a book of his photographs, since it might be my last year coaching. I did, and here I am writing this foreword for this great photography book that Andy has shot over the past season.

When the New York Knicks won their first championship in 1970, I collaborated with their photographer, George Kalinsky. We did a photography book called *Take It All!*, which was the unifying cry of those Knicks that playoff season. The book did well, and George went on to produce a number of photography books that were very successful.

Andy and I are not going to duplicate that book, which was just about the playoffs. We have our own style that will include a number of highlights or lowlights of the Lakers' entire 2009-10 NBA season. The one thing we did copy from *Take It All!*, however, was to make this a black and white photography book.

Andy used black and white for the documentary nature of the work in this book, reminiscent of the work of some of the greatest black and white documentary film photographers. For me, black and white photography has a depth to it that makes a softer, deeper quality picture, with textures of grays and shadows that really give life to the photograph. We hope it has a similar impact for you and the basketball fans across the NBA.

There are spaces and times in the season that bring different levels of intensity. Obviously, a team that has gone to the Finals and played the extra seven to eight weeks of basketball necessary to reach this point knows that the beginning of training camp is not where it reaches its zenith as a team. In this book Andy has shown the easy, casual, happy Lakers team from its beginning point to the angst and pain that comes at the end of those 114 or so games played to get to that final game, the end of that journey to the ring.

We have collaborated on giving the reader the best look at the inside of the game, from the locker rooms to the backstage activity in various arenas around the country. Don't worry! There are plenty of action shots inside the games, but these photos truly capture a story of more than just great athletic feats.

06.17.10 — LOS ANGELES

Hallelujah! The journey to the ring ends.

Kobe is relaxing at his locker in our training facility, the Toyota Center, before media day, also our first day of practice. Kobe had been active between seasons in 2007 and 2008 with the USA basketball team, which qualified for and eventually won the 2008 Olympics. He had a relaxing summer after pushing himself and the Olympic team the previous seasons. I had told Kobe after the 2007 qualifying rounds that his "job" as a Laker was to lead the team during games, but his days of leading the team during training camp and practices in the summer of '09 were limited. He has to care for his joints — knees, ankles, hips — as he enters the mature seasons of his career. Here he is enjoying the role of team spokesperson.

Training Camp

TRAINING CAMP BEGINS with media day, when the team is available to the local, national, and international press corps for photos and interviews. After the two-hour media event, we have a lengthy team meeting and then begin our first day of practice. This is one tough segment of the season. Players come into camp in all types of shape: guys who haven't played or worked out in the off-season, players who have had medical situations that prevented them from conditioning, players who have played on national teams, and players who are in the best shape possible without playing actual games. We went into the middle of June in the 2009 Finals, and now we are a little more than a hundred days away from the last game. So we're going to take it pretty easy this camp, because the goal is still more than seven months away.

Mitch Kupchak and I get together during the latter part of the summer and make sure we have a roster of close to twenty players. The new players are expected to come into camp and work hard and help get our team ready for the coming campaign. Some of them will find roster spots on other teams, sometimes in other countries, but my staff and I want them to have the full experience of Lakers basketball.

The camp is twenty-eight days, with the middle fourteen days spent playing seven games in Southern California and one in Las Vegas. We try to play a couple of back-to-back games to simulate the NBA schedule. The last week or so we have to get our roster down to a manageable limit and the team ready for the opening games. The players begin to shake off the effects of "boot camp" and ready themselves for the real thing.

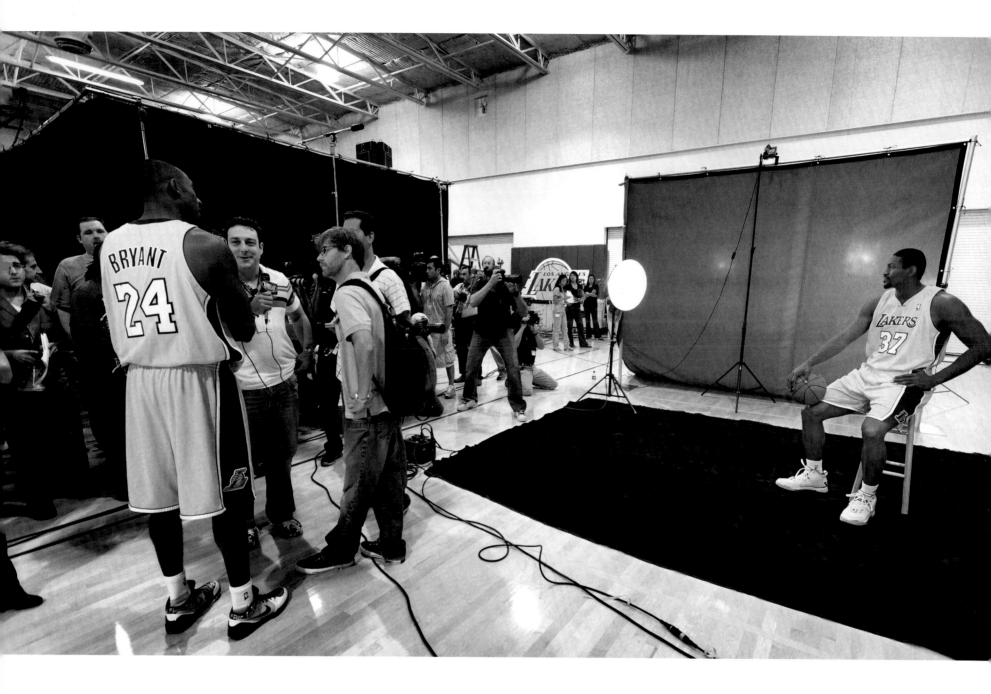

09.29.09 — EL SEGUNDO, CA

The media set up their stations for shots. Ron is at a station that requires NBA photos, while Kobe is next. Some members of the media have a chance to chat with Kobe "off the record." Kobe has an ability with the media to share his time and knowledge about the game with great ease. We usually map out a game plan for the media session with the players: what our goal is, who we see as our biggest challengers, and how we are going to get through the season to this end goal. The map doesn't always come out as we hope, but it gives us a message as a team. Ron has his mind on getting that ball from his knee to the basket.

09.29.09 — EL SEGUNDO, CA

This is Ron's second chance to speak as a Laker. Obviously, his first media session was after he signed as a free agent in July. There are plenty of media here to ask him how he came to be a Laker. Ron was in our locker room in Boston after the 2008 loss to the Celtics. He asked me whether he could talk to Kobe, who was taking a shower postgame. It was no secret that he wanted to join our club; the question was just the mechanics of how it could happen. The media like to talk to Ron. He's very entertaining and animated when he speaks. He said at this media session that he was here to help Kobe win another championship.

09.29.09 — EL SEGUNDO, CA

Before our first practice began four hours after the media session on the first official day of NBA training camp, Luke and Lamar chat. They had just finished a short workout with some weights prior to practice. Chip Shaefer is our physical trainer in charge of weight and conditioning amid other trivial things like taping ankles. He has the players on a schedule to work with weights before or after practices. LO is notorious about not working out during the summertime, but this summer he has, and his form was boxing as a conditioning activity. He looks fit to me. Luke and Lamar are the social guys on our team. They have a real community spirit about them — sometimes to a fault — creating a family feel most of the time.

10.01.09 — EL SEGUNDO, CA

Chip is bringing the guys through our first official function as a team. We take time to stretch before workouts. Sometimes we do a more dynamic stretch, but on the first day we go through the whole nine yards. My staff and I like to join the activity just to keep the process focused. I'm at my "chair" putting some finishing touches on a practice plan. As coaches, we have spent an hour before practice setting up the day's activity. We have two-and-a-half hours, including stretching, to put the players through their paces. Some days we focus more on defense and some on offense, but we have a lot to do in twenty-eight short days of work.

10.01.09 — EL SEGUNDO, CA

During this training camp Pau is given a pass to "go slow." His national team, Spain, had played in the European championship. The Spaniards ended up winning the tournament, which finished in mid-September. We want to start easy with Pau, but he ends up playing more than we want as DJ Mbenga comes into camp hurt. It costs us, as Pau pulls a hamstring and misses the first eleven games of the season. Here he is doing some Core X activities under the direction of Alex McKechnie, our talented physical therapist.

10.01.09 — EL SEGUNDO, CA

I have had to limit my time on the floor as a coach the past four years because of some physical disabilities, but Andy caught me on the floor going through an offensive sequence with Adam Morrison. Adam is a 3 (small forward), but I'm indicating that we're going through a three-pass option in the triangle offense.

10.01.09 — EL SEGUNDO, CA

[Left] There are times that I like to have Jeanie Buss open the shades in her office. It allows the players to view the nine trophies that Dr. Buss' teams have won over the past thirty years, through 2009. These trophies have become a symbol of NBA excellence and the dedication it takes to win them.

10.17.09 — LOS ANGELES

[Right] We start our preseason games. The players get their introduction acts ready. Derek Fisher is getting his traditional "low down" from his teammates.

10.18.09 — LOS ANGELES

The preseason game brings a mixture of opportunities for players who are vying for playing time, learning the triangle offense, or just learning how to play with their new teammates. I like to play the starters limited minutes, maybe sixteen to twenty-four minutes early in the preseason schedule and let everyone get a chance to perform. The vets often have a good time watching the action happening on court. Sometimes I'm not sure whether they are laughing with our players or about our players.

10.18.09 — LOS ANGELES

Pau gets used to a permanent seat during the preseason games. He and Luke will be there for most of the month of November. What I do like is that they stay involved. Pau is very supportive of his teammates and helps guys playing his position. I don't think he is just checking out the Laker Girls, who are also getting their routines down for the upcoming season.

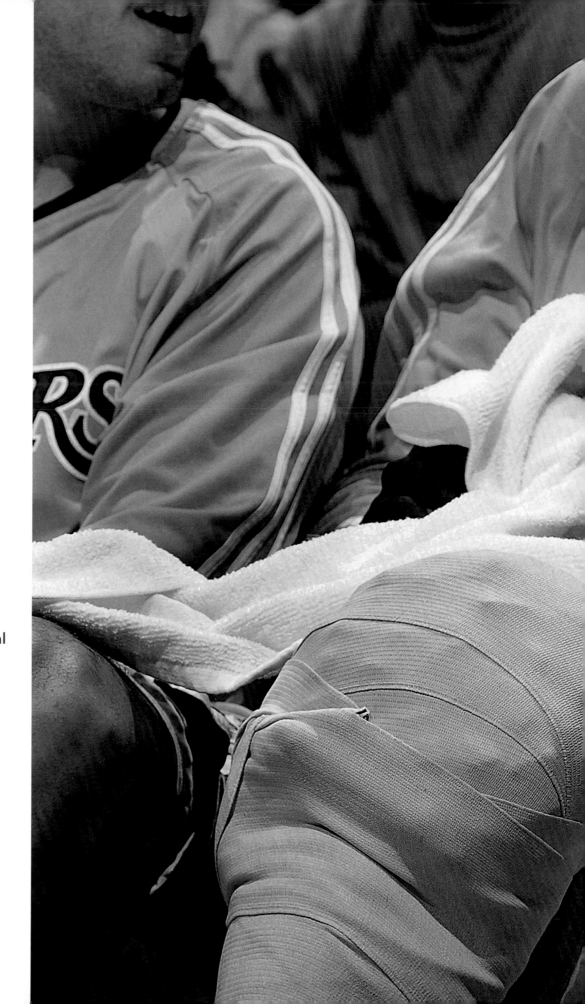

When the game is on ice, the players ice. It is almost habitual for players to ice their knees, and many ice their feet after a game. If the game has been decided and the starters are out, they always get their icing done as quickly as possible. The ice pack stays on for about twenty minutes. If they can get the icing done before they get to the locker room, it really shortens the night.

10.27.09 — LOS ANGELES

"Here we go, huh!" The players come out of the hallway by their locker room, ready to begin the new season. This is right after they huddle up in the hallway, and LO gives them a final challenge. The guys look as if they're ready to take on the world, or at least the NBA.

The Beginning

THE SEASON SCHEDULE, which is created by the NBA, becomes available in late summer, and we look at it with curiosity to understand what our travel year is going be like, or in what city against which team our holidays are going to be spent. Then in October the season starts, and we're playing into this schedule. The first game for us after winning the NBA championship, as we did in 2009, is a ring ceremony night. It is a game that sometimes gets lost in the final celebration of a championship that was won four months earlier. The rings are handed out, the players try them on, grinning like kids at Christmas, and then the ball boys come and take them from the players, and we get underway.

The early part of this season we have a couple of players who figure into our scheme of play who have become injured. Pau Gasol and Luke Walton start out the season with injuries, which puts pressure on our team. We have a generous home-weighted schedule at the beginning of this year, and we would like to take advantage of this opportunity.

After the warm-ups there is a five-minute break for the ring ceremony before the season opener against the Clippers. Usually the commissioner, David Stern, gives a short congratulatory talk and then announces the players receiving rings. Jeanie Buss, representing the Lakers, hands out the rings — she loves doing this public appearance — and Andy captures us. I think I should have kissed her! [Right] Kobe shows off his ring, while in the background LO and Pau examine their rings. There is a laser etching of each player on his ring. We won this game, 99-92.

11.01.09 — LOS ANGELES

Against Atlanta, we wanted to overwhelm the Hawks with Andrew's size. Since Pau is out, LO starts and Andrew becomes the focus of our attempts to get it inside. Drew is a very good scorer — he has a soft touch around the basket. Here he is using his jump hook to go over a double team by two Atlanta players.

11.01.09 — LOS ANGELES

After a timeout is called, the teams head off the court. While they are headed to the bench, Kobe is giving Ron some information about our offense. The players have about one minute of "free" time during a timeout before I come in to huddle the team. They are able to towel off, get a drink, and discuss the game. Sometimes we tell them to just be quiet and get focused. Then we huddle up and go over two or three things defensively and offensively in the last twenty seconds before we're back on the floor. This is a 118-110 win.

11.08.09 — LOS ANGELES

[Above] Lamar had a very busy summer. He had a whirlwind romance and ended up marrying Khloe Kardashian the weekend before training camp. Then LO has to jump right into action when the season starts as Pau is on the sidelines because of a hamstring injury. This shot is from our game versus New Orleans, a 104-88 win. [Below] Here's what Lamar's shoes look like. He writes these two names on his shoes before every game. It's LO's tribute to his loved ones who have passed on.

11.15.09 — LOS ANGELES

Players gather in
the hallway before
a game against the
Houston Rockets.
Every player has his
own ritual before
the team gathers
and goes into its
pregame huddle.
Usually the whole
team impatiently
awaits Sasha
Vujacic, our most
ritualistic player,
while he does his
last-minute prayer.

After the introductions, the players get their warm-ups off and do their last-minute details before coming into the huddle before the tip-off. I'm on the sidelines, writing down the matchups (sometimes there are last-minute changes in lineups) and usually the first two options for the game. Sometimes we like to use a tip-off rush, because of the size of our centers and to set a tone for the game. Most of the time, we want to get the ball inside to our big guys to get a chance to read the defensive plan of our opponents. Often, teams will have a strategy to front the post or double-team the post player. We want to get adjusted to those strategies right out of the blocks. This game we lost, 101-91, to Houston.

11.22.09 — LOS ANGELES

Andrew Bynum comes off the floor after a 101-85 victory over Oklahoma City. The family seats are right behind the bench and many of the players get personal high-fives or verbal support from their families and friends. The trip to the locker room is accompanied by shout-outs from spectators. On the road, it is a chance for the hometown fans to hurl insults at the players and coaches as they walk off the floor, and here at home you can see the support our fans want to lavish on one of their favorites. This photo Andy took truly shows the size of Staples — notice the banners of the Lakers' all-time greats on the wall of fame.

11.26.09 — PLAYA DEL REY, CA

Ah, yes, it's turkey time — one of my favorite times of year. I collaborate with my daughter, Brooke, and her family to make the Thanksgiving dinner. Brooke is a terrific cook, and she is doing all the vegetables and assorted things that make dinner great. I've been charged with doing the turkey and then carving it up — the easy part. The best part of Thanksgiving Day is when we stop before or during dinner and recount our blessings. We have so much to be grateful for and just a couple of hours before this shot I told my players that I was thankful for them, just before we had one of our lighter practices: the Turkey Trot.

12.02.09 — EL SEGUNDO, CA

Ron tweeted his fans to meet him on the beach for some touch football. He loves reaching out to the Twitter followers and engaging them on his joy ride of playing in the NBA.

The Long Home Stand Continues

OUTSIDE OF A two-game trip to Oklahoma City and Houston, we have a home-court advantage by playing seventeen of our first twenty-one games at Staples Center. We have a road game in Denver on November 13 after playing host to Phoenix the night before, a November 28 game at Golden State, a five-game road swing before Christmas, and only two other games away from Staples Center before January 8, a wildly unbalanced home-court diet. Of our first thirty-four games, twenty-three are at home. We win twenty of them (and eight on the road).

I feel fine about it; we'd like to get some momentum for the season by winning a lot of these home games early on. The fact that Pau is injured and missing a good portion of the month of November doesn't help us reap all the benefits of this home stand, but we play well enough to begin the year in a positive way. We get trounced in Denver after beating our closest rival Phoenix the night before. It is one of those schedule losses one has to resist falling prey to; I hit the sack in Denver as the bedside clock says 4 a.m. We score a measly 23 points in the second half that night versus the Nuggets. People see Denver as the team that will challenge us in the West.

The game that everyone has pointed to on our schedule is the Christmas Day game versus Cleveland. It proves to be a terrible day for us at Staples. They not only beat us, but do it handily and enjoy it a whole lot. Our fans have a bad day, and after a disputed call against Kobe, they lob some of their #1 big fingers onto the court. It's not dangerous, but it uncharacteristic for Lakers fans.

12.05.09 — EL SEGUNDO, CA

This photo was taken at our team's annual holiday party for children. Each year, about a hundred kids from local nonprofit youth organizations are invited to spend a fun-filled afternoon with the team and Laker Girls. The children play video and carnival games with them, participate in arts and crafts projects, get autographs, and receive presents at the end of the party.

A couple of practices a year are open to spectators. One, for our box holders, is usually held at the Toyota Center in El Segundo, and another, for a sponsor, American Express, is held at Staples Center. This practice is an opportunity for us to play on our home court. Since we share this court with the Kings and the Clippers, and Staples is the busiest arena in the country, it is to our advantage to practice as often as we can in the arena where we play.

12.08.09 — WESTWOOD, CA

One of the toughest
appearances for players, and
one of the most rewarding,
is to visit kids in hospitals.
Pau Gasol, who once went
to medical school and hoped
to be a doctor, has the grace
and ability to talk to children
about medical treatment
and bring some joy into their
lives. Here he is engaging
with a boy named Jesse at
Mattel Children's Hospital
UCLA, bringing him a ball
and those notorious fingers
that ended up on the floor
after our Christmas Day game
versus the Cleveland Cavs.

12.09.09 — LOS ANGELES

In the pregame introduction, the starting five are announced with much fanfare and then our bench players go into their pregame routine. They usually get in a circle, put one player in the middle, and rally around him. These rituals have evolved over the years, giving the bench players a way to be involved and catch the fever of the game. I'm just an observer, but I appreciate their team spirit.

12.11.09 — LOS ANGELES

Near mid-December, we play the Minnesota Timberwolves, coached by Kurt Rambis. Kurt was an important part of our coaching staff the previous year, and we take a moment before the game to honor his contribution to the Lakers by presenting him his championship ring. Kurt brought his offbeat sense of humor to work and was our defensive coordinator during our run for the 2008-09 championship.

Andy got this shot of a young fan, who has the chance to sit on the sideline next to the Lakers' bench. LO gives these kids a once-over: "Hey, is that kid texting during the game? We'd get busted if we did this."

12.11.09 — LOS ANGELES

Game 21 vs. the Minnesota Timberwolves ... This is a team that knows us and our triangle offense really well as it's coached by Kurt Rambis. Their strategy in this game is to drop off Lamar and sit in front of Pau, so LO can't pass the ball into the post. You can tell the kind of respect players have for Gasol by the intensity of this defense. We won this game 104-92.

01.03.10 — LOS ANGELES

Ron holds court in front of
his locker before a game.
There is a period of forty-five
minutes before each game that
the media have access to an
NBA locker room. European
sportswriters have mentioned
how astounded they are at
this policy. Most of the players
retreat to the training room, go
into our lounge, or are out on
the court shooting before the
game to avoid this open forum.

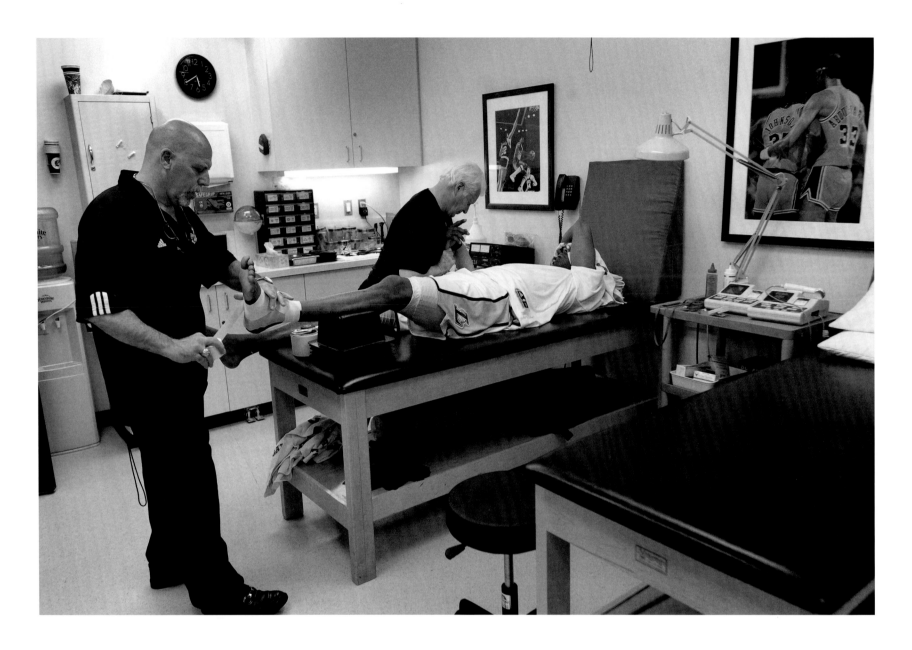

01.03.10 — LOS ANGELES

This is the training room at Staples Center. Here two trainers, Gary Vitti and Alex McKechnie, are working on Kobe. Gary is taping his ankle, and Alex is mobilizing Kobe's hand. There are four trainers going full-out, for an hour and a half before every game. Usually there are two guys taping, one working with mobilization techniques, and one doing some supervised powerlifting before games.

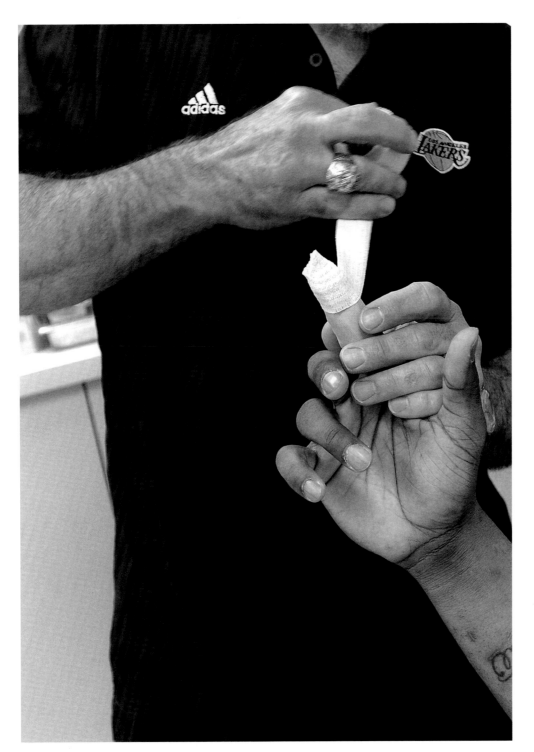

01.03.10 — LOS ANGELES

The finger ... Kobe breaks his finger in the Minnesota game December 11. It is just an errant pass, or he doesn't quite reach far enough to get the ball, and it hits off the end of his finger and breaks the bone. For the rest of the year, that finger would go through a variety of taping procedures, just one of the many injuries Kobe endured during the season. He played through this "minor" problem, adjusting his shot to accommodate the taped finger.

01.07.10 — TEAM PLANE

We're on the plane. Guys are creatures of habit and they sit near teammates with whom they can share music and movies. Kobe and I sit across from each other, and Fish sits just in front of Kobe. This is to our advantage. There are times when we are in the air that we can watch game video or confer with each other about game situations.

Traveling Music

AFTER A LONG home stand, we are ready to hit the road. We have a cluster of shorter trips before we head out on an eight-game trip. This trip extends from January to the beginning of February. You have to pay the piper, and we have had a chance to get off to a great start, mostly on the benefit of our long home stand.

The long trip includes Cleveland with major stops in New York, Washington, and Boston, before we end up with a conference opponent in Memphis. The Cleveland game is another disappointing outing against the Cavs. LeBron James engineers a comeback that we couldn't match.

We were hoping for a great trip, but after starting with the Cleveland loss, another close game in Toronto sullies the trip. We gain a little ground after our White House visit with a win versus the Wiz and then top it off with a one-point victory in Boston. The victory against the Celtics is a seesaw game in which we start off with a bang only to have them bounce back in the second quarter and shut us down. Late in the game, Kobe finds his touch, Andrew puts in a hoop, Kobe adds free throws, Ron makes a shot and draws an offensive foul on Paul Pierce, and then Kobe drops in the winner. Whew! We head out that afternoon for a back-to-back game in Memphis. The chance to celebrate a victory or lament a loss is always followed by another game soon.

01.07.10 — PORTLAND

When we land, usually two buses drive out to meet us. One bus is for the players, trainers, and the staff, and one bus is for the media group. We are very lucky to travel by a chartered service.

01.07.10 — PORTLAND

When we pull up to the hotel, it doesn't matter what time of night or whether we've changed the venue, there is a group of autograph seekers waiting for us to arrive. The players (Lamar and Luke here) on short trips pull their own bags out of the bus and get to their rooms. In this photo, you can see it is during the dark days of winter by the tree lights of downtown Portland.

01.08.10 — PORTLAND

Boarding the bus to go to a shootaround practice in Portland, Oregon ... Josh Powell pauses before getting on the bus to sign an autograph. The hotels usually have a spot close to the bus for fans to gather to watch the players board the bus. The autograph seekers are almost magical in their ability to find out our next move. Sometimes I change the location of our "shoot," and the fan corps will beat us to our next stop even if it's off the map — it's almost psychic.

In the morning, if we are in the same time zone, we have a shootaround in the arena where we will play in seven to eight hours. At times, we will abort a shootaround if we get into a city past 2 a.m. or if the travel to the arena is too long. We divide into groups of players. The "bigs" on one end of the court work on their inside game via our offense, and, at the other end, the "smalls" are doing the same thing, but taking longer jump shots.

01.08.10 — PORTLAND

Ron at the shootaround ... Don't ask me what he's doing, but it looks as if he's getting his hands ready and comfortable with the ball. Ron plays much of his defense with his hands — he's quick and strong with his hands — and this season he had a severe injury to his thumb. He had to tape his fingers and thumb before shooting. Ron has just gotten back with the team after missing five games because of a concussion.

01.08.10 — PORTLAND

So far, this season has been a bust for Luke. He has had back spasms. This has been a problem in the past, and the past two seasons it's a big concern. He has gone through some medical procedures to quiet the nerves, and now is back on his rehab program with Alex. These exercises are part of the Core X therapy program Alex has developed to recover the core strength necessary for these athletes to perform at the highest levels. Luke has now become part of the coaching staff, he has been out so long.

At the end of our shootaround practice, the players go through a round of free throws. During this time, they get "personal" with each other, kidding and horsing around. We often give them incentive goals to bring more focus to their free throws. One never knows when a free throw may be at the most critical part of the game. Here, at the guard end of the court, Kobe, Jordan, and Shannon exchange barbs.

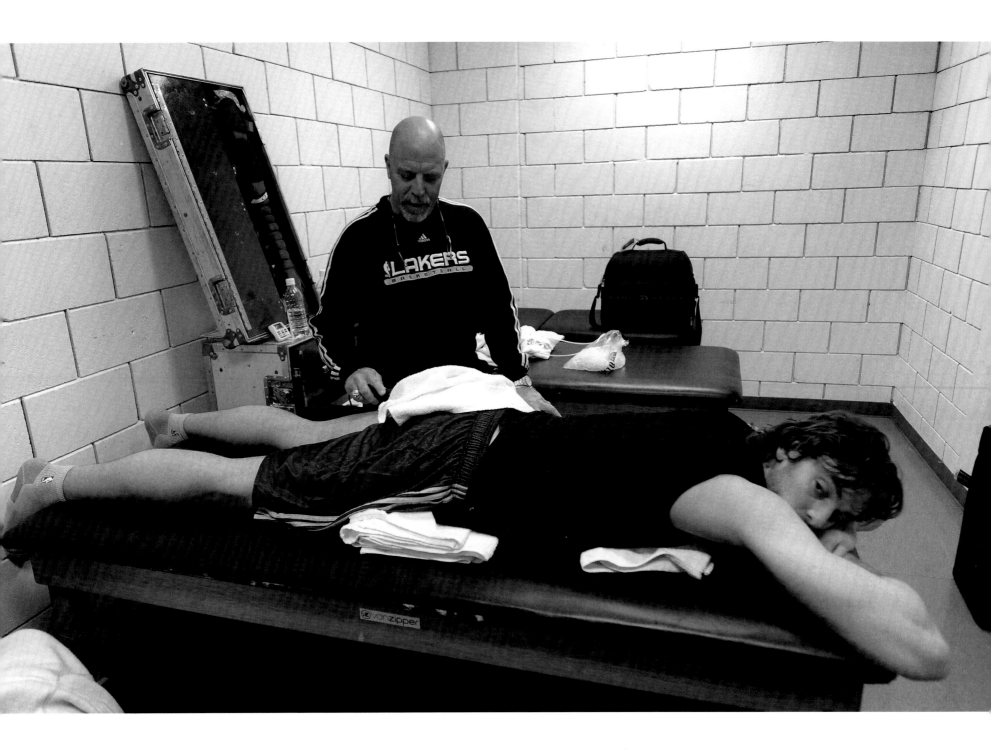

Yes, here is Pau's favorite place in the locker room — the training table. Notice how relaxed and comfortable he is in this position. Gary Vitti is giving him some ultrasound stimulation on his hamstring. Pau has had problems on and off since training camp with his hamstrings, and after missing the first eleven games he had another "hammy." He needs to go through a procedure during our shootaround to prevent another injury.

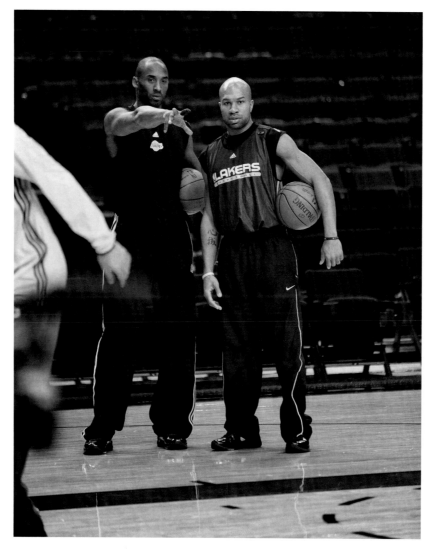

01.08.10 — PORTLAND

[Above] After we finish the shooting part of
our morning practice, we go through some
strategy stations in preparation for our opponent.
Against Portland, it is important that we know
how to attack the Trail Blazers' defense. Kobe
and Derek are talking about the spacing on the
floor for our triangle offense. After the players
leave the court, Luke and Alex work on Luke's
conditioning. It's a lonely time for a player,
and our trainers try to make it challenging.

Here is the crowd of fans a player has to walk through back at the hotel. Kobe has his hands full here as he is one of the key players the autograph seekers love to pursue. By and large, these people are friendly and work at the challenge of getting their autographs. It never fails to amuse me how they find out where we are staying and where we are going.

01.08.10 — PORTLAND

Going up? ... It's a daring soul who would want to get on that elevator. The players are notorious gangsters on elevators, but that's usually because someone gets on and can't quite deal with six to eight guys on a car who are all 6 feet 6 inches or taller. "What are you guys, a basketball team?" So then the jokes begin: "No, we're a ..." You can insert anything in here "circus/elephant jockeys/ environmentalists/dancers." I've heard them all.

01.08.10 — PORTLAND

Here is one of our warriors, Josh Powell, after our morning practice, getting ready to head on back to the bus. You can see he's fully equipped. His knees are bagged and getting iced, and his hoodie is on, and he has his ubiquitous headphones back on his head.

Josh has been a valuable asset to our team. Even though he plays limited minutes, he is always involved and ready to do what he can for the team.

01.21.10 — CLEVELAND

After the early practices, we coaches often find time to talk to our players about key factors in the upcoming contest. Pau and I are discussing where his release point is in his hook shot. He has a couple of releases on his hook shot. I like it when it's shot not just as a floater, because he has such length to go over the top, and he can absorb the contact to make adjustments. Pau is a great player, but it comes so easy to him I like to keep him focused on his game and getting even better.

The bowels of the arenas are always different. A lot of times the seating and floor spacing are very similar, but how one gets to the locker room and court is never the same. This is Cleveland's arena. In about six hours, this space will be filled with fans. Sometimes it's not easy to walk through the fans after a game, especially when things have not worked out well on the court. Sasha's checking out his iPhone just to see what he's missed while at practice.

01.22.10 — NEW YORK CITY

The locker of Kobe Bryant ... The equipment manager, Rudy Garciduenas, sets up the locker room while we are out on the court in the morning shootarounds. This spot I know well — it's the Knicks' visitors locker room. Each player has his grouping or space to hang out getting dressed. Notice the shoes, shower shoes, valuables bag, and the unusual item on the floor is an Achilles stretch board.

01.22.10 — NEW YORK CITY

Madison Square Garden has an entrance through a parking space to an elevator that takes equipment and the teams up to the fifth floor. It's slow, and sometimes one has to share it with the garbage coming down to ground level. It's big enough for the elephants, let alone a basketball team. Once out of this elevator, where the players are heading, you meet the horde of reporters waiting for the team's entrance into this magical arena.

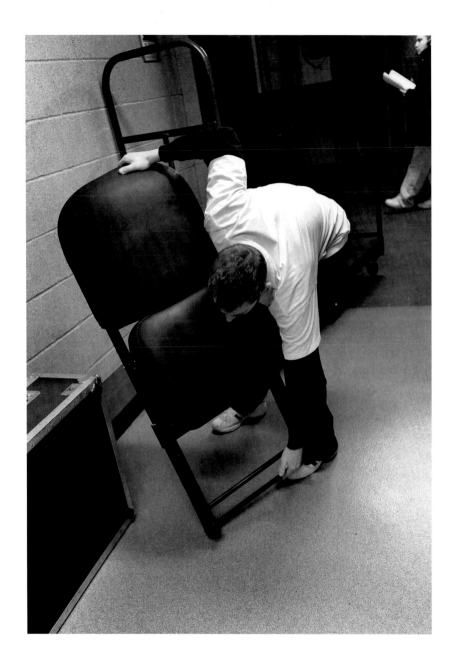

The Chair! Rudy hauls it all over the country, so I
can sit at the appropriate level for my height on the
court. It's been ridiculed, but a number of teams have
begun to use one. The portable courts are raised
about six inches off the floor, so when we tall guys sit
in a normal chair, our knees come up to our chests,
which can create back problems. Good for me.

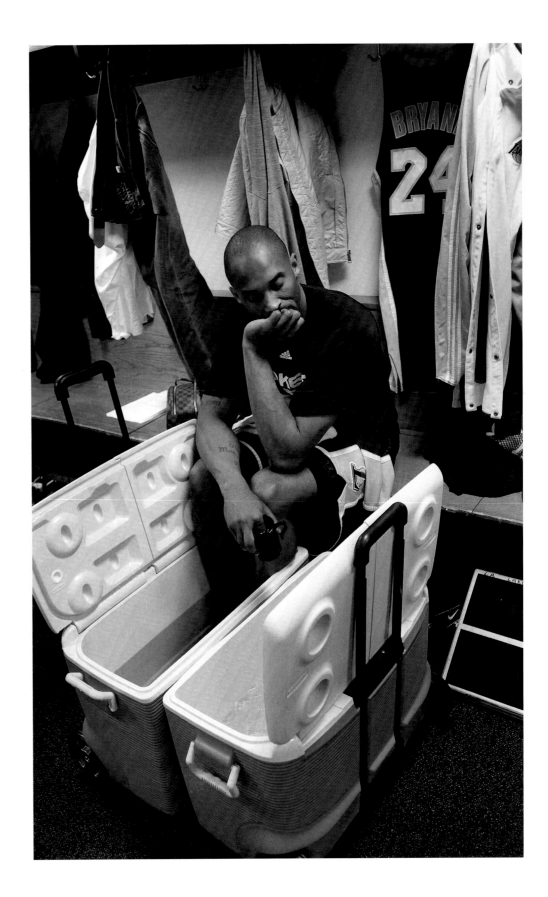

01.22.10 — NEW YORK CITY

Ritual before the game ... Kobe sits with his feet in ice water. You can see he has a small cup with ice for his finger. This is not Rodin's *Thinker*, but he's thinking ... Thinking about the game, or his opponent and how to measure up to the challenge. Last year he put 61 points on the Knicks. They will be ready to play a different defense on this night and maybe try to double-team him.

01.23.10 — TORONTO

At the Four Seasons Hotel in Toronto, DJ is changing his U.S. money for some local currency. This year's trip to Canada has come with a day between games, and Canadian dollars will be needed. Notice the Haitian disaster relief box is calling for DJ to drop some of that money in the slot. The earthquake in Port-au-Prince had just happened.

With a day between games, the players who didn't play more than twenty minutes in the New York game are required to "get a sweat." We also have volunteers who come to join in, but with back-to-back games the previous nights in Cleveland and New York, the starters are looking forward to a day off. Jordan leads the pack down the hallway to the bus. They will be greeted by the most eclectic bus-meeting fans in the NBA.

01.23.10 — TORONTO

This is the first part of the workout the guys go through on days off. Each player has a weight or strength program that fits his particular needs. They do a number of lifts, mostly with free weights rather than on machines. Shannon is getting the most out of some shoulder presses. Sasha is going through a Core X workout. He has to keep on top of some core issues that manifest themselves in back problems. After the players are finished with their strength and therapy workouts, they head to the court for b-ball.

01.25.10 — WASHINGTON, D.C.

The visit to the White House was a major moment of our road trip. The players all look very attentive posing with President Obama. Pau's hair even looks coiffed. On the right, Magic, Mitch Kupchak, and Jeanie Buss stood in with the team. We were given spots to occupy from the smalls to the bigs. Which is why I've been placed in left field instead of standing next to Jeanie, although Adam Morrison *is* a great guy.

01.26.10 — WASHINGTON, D.C.

In the hallway at the Verizon Center in D.C. ... We played the night after the awards ceremony in the White House. This has been one of our best stops on any trip for the past couple of years. This photo shows the players getting their last-minute stretches before the team huddles on its way to the court, about a two-minute walk from the locker room.

01.26.10 — WASHINGTON, D.C.

This is the final walk before heading out onto the court. The fans lean over the railing and give a shout-out to their favorite players. This game is just a couple of weeks after the Gilbert Arenas firearm discovery. This was a very discouraged Wizards team and franchise after that disclosure. Hopefully, they will get back in the hunt, as many people thought they had made good progress in forming their roster for the season. We won!

A mile marker on the journey comes on February 3, Lakers versus Charlotte. This victory at Staples Center gives me more wins — 534 — as a coach of the Lakers than the former coach, Pat Riley. It really is a team thing, which includes the staff I've worked with over the years: Tex Winter, Jim Cleamons, Frank Hamblen, Brian Shaw, Bill Bertka, and Kurt Rambis. The wins come and so do the losses; it's about championships that teams win.

The Dog Days

THE ALL-STAR BREAK is a period in the season when everyone stops playing and we let the stars do the work. For the Lakers, we have a five-day break and try to get our lives back to normal. The season resumes with two home games, one of them against Boston, and then we go on the road again. We have a few longer-type trips left. One is to the East with Miami, Charlotte, and Orlando yet to be played, and we have a longer-type trip in our conference during the Pac-10 tournament when we vacate Staples. Packing bags and moving daily as you travel the country starts to get old. One of my coaches used to say: "The dogs bark, the women cry, but the caravan moves on."

Since early in the season, Kobe has been playing with injuries. The season wear-and-tear finally gets the best of him, and he has to miss games. This is something we pride ourselves on — playing all the games. There is a saying: "If it hurts you can play; if it's broken you can sit."

Obviously, this doesn't apply to torn ligaments and tendons, but, for the most part, players play with pain. Kobe finally has one too many injuries and sits out games February 6 through 18. We play on, winning four of five games, losing only to the Celtics in a close game, but the toll has its effect down the line. We slide into the month of April, ready for playoffs to start.

02.03.10 — LOS ANGELES

Kobe Bryant and Jerry West pose for a
ceremonial photo after Jerry's record of
25,192 points as a Laker was surpassed by
Kobe on February 1. Jerry was instrumental
in getting Kobe to the Lakers and was
personally invested in Kobe's success. It's
quite a story, and then to have Kobe best
his scoring record in the process makes
a very personal triumph for both men.

02.05.10 — LOS ANGELES

Kobe is getting ready to attack Arron Afflalo of the Denver Nuggets. The game against Denver was our second loss of the season to the Nuggets. Chauncey Billups hit nine three-point shots in this game. We are very concerned about our matchups versus Denver. They are painting themselves to be our challengers in the West in the playoffs. Less than two weeks later their coach, George Karl, would announce that he was going to undergo radiation therapy for cancer.

02.05.10 — LOS ANGELES

The games against the Nuggets bring potent matchups. Derek Fisher versus Chauncey Billups and Ron Artest against Carmelo Anthony. Here Derek gets ready to use his footwork or maybe "step-back" to a shot in the game. We were feeling as if it were "dog days" in the NBA after this loss, 126-113. Needless to say, we don't appreciate any team winning on our home court or getting the season series advantage against us.

02.05.10 — LOS ANGELES

The battle in the lane features Lamar going up against Kenyon Martin, while Pau is trying to get position on Nenê. The Nuggets have one of the strongest front lines in the game, even though they give up some height. In the past two playoffs, we have won with our big men scoring in the lane and with Kobe's scoring prowess. This season they have geared their team up to try to match our strengths.

02.05.10 — LOS ANGELES

Andrew Bynum gets a breather during the game ... We like to play Andrew in stages of eight to nine minutes if possible. Keeping him fresh and eager to play really allows him to give us a big impact. Usually we lead off with an emphasis on our size and Andrew is the one who usually gives us that punch. You can see the details of his brace — those are valuable knees.

02.18.10 — LOS ANGELES

The clock says 9:50 p.m. The game is in the fourth quarter versus the Celtics, and Kobe is getting therapy in the training room while watching the game. This photo was taken while the interview of the home court coach (me) was being shown on the TV. I wonder whether Kobe's grin is about the game or the interview. This is the fifth game Kobe has been out and we lose a close one this night, 87–86.

02.18.10 — LOS ANGELES

Going down the lane against the Celtics is a challenge. They have shot blockers, and they are also good at taking charges in the lane. Here Ron is past Paul Pierce and has to take on Kevin Garnett to get to the hoop. Lurking in the background is Kendrick Perkins trying to get in on the action. During the time Kobe was out, we had won four games in succession with Shannon Brown picking up the starting role and Sasha Vujacic backing him up.

02.18.10 — LOS ANGELES

Fourth-quarter action against the Celtics, trying to get the lead back ... Here we are defending a screen/roll play. You can see that the bench is involved in the defensive play and giving vocal support to our players. The Celtics won this one, evening out the series after we had beaten them on their home court. It was a harbinger of things to come in the playoffs in June.

02.20.10 — EL SEGUNDO, CA

Kobe working on his game with Craig Hodges, our shooting coach ... The effort it takes to come back after sitting for a couple of weeks is shown in this photo. It requires dedication to strengthening the body, treating the damaged tissue, and then reestablishing your game. Here is a symbolic photo of what it takes to win these trophies. Above, at a shooting break during practice, I am diagramming a special situation.

02.20.10 — EL SEGUNDO, CA

"OK, you guys in white are going to run this sequence while our guys in blue are going to defend it." This is probably pretty close to what is being said here as we prepare for a game against an opponent. Practice includes getting in sync with each other inside our triangle offense, getting our shooting touch down, and practicing how to defend the upcoming opponents.

02.20.10 — EL SEGUNDO, CA

The brace ... Andrew has several of these braces. Here he straps on his brace before we go into the "contact" part of practice. He needs to have a number of braces because the coach will occasionally mistake the brace for a pile of towels and kick it in anger. Andrew has one for practice and a couple he takes to games. They are a protective measure and they help.

02.20.10 — EL SEGUNDO, CA

This picture is taken in Jeanie's office with the trophies in the background. You can see that a couple of trophies are missing. At this time, the Lakers have won nine championships during Dr. Buss' ownership, but we hope there are more to come. One thing, the pile on the desk is not how my desk looks. I keep mine cleared off.

Here is a segment of the practice that the players usually enjoy the most, the chance to scrimmage against each other. Josh Powell is all over Andrew's shot in the first photo even though he gives up about five inches to Drew. Kobe is preparing to make his comeback after being out for five games, and you can see the sleeve on the knee. The second photo is Shannon baiting Andrew to block his floater in the lane. The reason a team improves during the year is because the reserves challenge starters in practice.

The marriage of Lamar to Khloe Kardashian brought about a change in LO's lifestyle. He moved to the Valley and started living the life of a married family man. Here he is parked on a lounge after a practice, relaxing with the daily newspaper. Looks as if he has the life of Riley.

The rematch! After a spanking on our home court by Denver, we get a chance to even things out late in the season. This is a game in an 82-game season that everyone puts a star next to because it has meaning for the playoffs. We needed this win to square things with the Nuggets as we go down the home stretch. LO's here putting a body on Kenyon Martin waiting for the rebound while Ron adds some strong-arm to the battle.

02.28-10 — LOS ANGELES

Nice to have Kobe back on the court, right? Here Pau gives Kobe a hug after a sequence of plays that put this Denver game in the "W" column, 95-89. Carmelo walks off the court after a discouraging sequence of events, having fouled out with 2:13 left in the fourth quarter.

03-02-10 — LOS ANGELES

The spoils of victory ... It's the time the starters can sit on the bench, ice, and enjoy the reserves finishing a game. Chick used to say: "This game's in the refrigerator: the door is closed, the lights are out, the eggs are cooling, the butter's getting hard, and the jello's jigglin'!" The finish to our season isn't the way we had hoped, but rising to the challenge in a game like this (defeating the Pacers, 122-99) gives us confidence we can reignite our game.

03.21.10 — LOS ANGELES

Kobe is answering questions at the Lakers' Fan Jam, a two-day weekend event held every year at the Los Angeles Convention Center. All the players go there to spend a half hour or more with the fans who also can get autographs signed by their favorite current and past Lakers players, see the Laker Girls, and test their own basketball skills in games and contests. It has become a very popular event with our fans, right next to Staples Center.

03.21.10 — LOS ANGELES

These are audience members at the Fan Jam, waiting for Kobe to come down off the podium and sign autographs. The event happens within the last couple of weeks of the season's end. It is priced low so that a lot of fans who might not be able to see a game get a chance to be with their favorite players.

04.18.10 — LOS ANGELES

Getting everything just right for the playoffs ... Kobe takes extra free throws before the first playoff game versus the Oklahoma City Thunder. Everything does matter in the playoffs.

Playoffs
First Round: Oklahoma City

OK, OKLAHOMA, OKAY! This is a team I did not want to see in the playoffs. It is on the rise as a young team. The last two weeks of the schedule play havoc in the West, as teams change positions almost nightly. Finally, after the dust settles, Oklahoma comes in eighth, winning fifty games — quite an accomplishment for a young team.

The series begins with us jumping ahead in the first quarter of the first game, elevating our game defensively and setting a tone for the opponent. They fight back but never get their star, Kevin Durant, untracked as we win the game, 87–79. They never lead in the game, but show us some pretty feisty defense. Even though we win Game 2, they are prepared and let us know they are going to give us a run, which they do, winning both games back in Oklahoma City. Their home crowd is a factor, as strange as that seems, but it is devoted fans that energize the Thunder. In the two games, they outscore us 47–9 on fast breaks.

Their strategy: Let Ron Artest shoot from the corner and run out on his misses, and boy, do they ever. Ron is 3 for 23 on three-pointers the first four games. It sets up an interesting scenario for the rest of the playoffs.

We make some changes in Game 5, the critical game in a seven-game series. Kobe tells me after Game 3: "I'm guarding Russell Westbrook!" I am good with that change, but I think it might limit his offense chasing the Young Turk around the court. It does change the series. We bomb them at home, leading at one point by 32 points with Kobe getting only 13, but Pau and Drew score more than 20 points each. Game 6 is one of those games good teams find a way to win. We do, with a put-back by Pau on Kobe's shot to win by one point. This was one tough series for us.

04.18.10 — LOS ANGELES

The pregame media ritual with the coaches goes from the hallways of arenas to a media room to a makeshift auditorium. This just gets larger and more involved as the playoffs continue. Before this round of the playoffs, I was fined by the league for allegedly putting "spin" on some issues regarding Kevin Durant's number of foul shots — he shot the most in the league and also led the league in scoring. Here I'm trying to downplay the issue.

04.20.10 — LOS ANGELES

The matchup of the series:
Kevin Durant vs. Ron Artest.
Here, in Game 2, Kevin is
trying to shed Ron before
running through some
screens. Shooters try to get
their defenders to stop or
push off to get some space
to make their teammates'
screens effective. Kevin is
good at this tactic, and Ron
is determined not to let him
"escape" or get called for a
foul. The key is to tailgate your
opponent around this traffic.

04.30.10 — OKLAHOMA CITY

[Above] The timeout: The players are back on the bench, and I know that look from Kobe. He's unhappy about a call on the floor in Game 6. Playoff games take on a much greater sense of urgency.

04.27.10 — LOS ANGELES

[Left] The national anthem is that momentary break before the action starts. Just about every person on our staff has a ritual he performs while the anthem is sung or played. Here it looks as if Kobe is getting all his reserves together for Game 5.

04.30.10 — OKLAHOMA CITY

The discussions between coaches and referees are often contentious, but I try to keep them on an even keel. There is a coaches box that we are supposed to observe, but many coaches disregard the line and come to half-court to argue their case. Here I am at half-court with the official, Kenny Mauer, trying to get the rationale for a call on the floor.

04.30.10 — OKLAHOMA CITY

The consolation after winning or losing a series is usually very heartfelt between the players. This series with the young Thunder was very hard-fought. We won this game 95-94 on their home court after a last-second put-back by Gasol. Here Pau is consoling Thunder guard Russell Westbrook, who had an outstanding series. Oklahoma City has a bright future with its Thunder. They will be heard from in the coming years.

05.07.10 — TEAM PLANE

We won the first two games
of the Utah series at home —
not easily — and now it's time
to go face the music at the
Jazz's home court. Here I am
heading up the stairway to the
plane. Notice my hat. This is
not the cap commemorating
the X title, but a cap that
Eddie Vedder gave me
commemorating Pearl
Jam's album #9 ... their
first album was called X.

Western Conference Semifinals: Utah

THIS OPPONENT ALMOST seems like a yearly struggle for us. The Jazz, one of the most disciplined teams in the NBA, make some changes during the season and revitalize their team around Deron Williams, a talented point guard, and Carlos Boozer, their scoring/rebounding big man. We know this team but seldom dominate them. They have the best shooting percentage in the NBA, most points scored in the lane, and make the most assists of any team in the league.

We again are "supposed" to win, as the Jazz have lost their starting center, Mehmet Okur, and their forward, Andrei Kirilenko, a very good defensive player, is limited by injury. In the series with Oklahoma City, Andrew Bynum has torn a ligament in his knee. He has some swelling and discomfort, but he wants to continue playing. We know our big men are a problem for the Jazz, but without Drew at full strength, Pau and Lamar have to pick up their games. We play two close games at home and win them by five and eight points, respectively.

Then we go on to Utah where they also have a devoted, rabid crowd. It is one of the most intimidating arenas in the league, with seats right at the baseline and sidelines. In Game 3, their bench comes to the rescue. Kyle Korver goes 9 for 10, making 5 for 5 three-point shots. Kirilenko comes off the bench to help, Paul Millsap gets 13 points, and we barely win by a point in a game that has twenty-two lead changes. Fish hits a three-pointer to give us a 109-108 lead with 28 seconds left, and then, in a wild finish, we escape after a turnover gives Utah a chance to win at the buzzer. Whew! The 111-110 win was a very devastating loss to the Jazz, and we finish off the series on their home court.

05.08.10 — SALT LAKE CITY

"Putting a stop on Booz"
... Here, Pau and Lamar trap Carlos Boozer at a critical juncture of Game 3 in Utah. Notice how Carlos is trying to create room to move by hooking his left elbow against Pau. Carlos has been one of the most productive forwards in the NBA the past four seasons, but we have been able to withstand his productivity.

05.08.10 — SALT LAKE CITY

The size and activity of Pau is a big reason we win in four games. Here in Game 3, Pau finds an easy tap-in over a smaller Kyle Korver and Paul Millsap. Pau later adds a remarkable game against Utah in Game 4 to clinch the series. He scores 33 points, making 12 of 18 shots, a big relief to us after his 14 points in Game 3. The Jazz run out of big men after injuries to Mehmet Okur and Andrei Kirilenko.

The joy of victory and the
frustration of defeat are shown
on the faces of the Lakers,
Kobe and Pau, and Utah's
Carlos Boozer. Game 3 is a
big win for us in Utah, but
it doesn't come easy as we
fritter away our lead at the
end of the game. The Jazz
have a chance to win but miss
a shot and a tip-in at the
buzzer before Pau rebounds
the missed tip opportunity
by Wesley Matthews.

The bus trip to our practice in Salt Lake ... Mitch Kupchak is giving the players the chance to board first before he puts his 6-foot 10-inch body in a bus seat. The ritual of boarding the bus is almost habitual — some guys are early, some are late. Kobe waits till the last moment to board the bus to avert the fan jam at the bus door.

05.09.10 — SALT LAKE CITY

What is this? The cat that ate the canary? That's what it looks like. Here Kobe's smiling that grin as he watches the morning practice. We had to cut back on the amount of work Kobe did outside of games after the Oklahoma City series. But he has time after his therapy to go through our defensive and offensive preparation.

05.09.10 — SALT LAKE CITY

The questions about strategy abound as the series goes forward. In this series, Utah had one starter out (Mehmet Okur) and another one (Andrei Kirilenko) who was questionable. Mitch and I exchange possibilities while the players warm up at the practice. Mitch and our team doctor, Steve Lombardo, travel with the team during our playoffs.

05.09.10 — SALT LAKE CITY

Luke makes one of his signature passes to his teammate during a practice in Salt Lake on our day off between Games 3 and 4. We usually have a short practice between games on the road just to get a workout for players who haven't had "big" minutes in the last game. This is part of a scrimmage at the end of practice. We often play three-on-three or four-on-four if we are short-handed due to long minutes to starters or injured players. The competitions can keep a player in sync and sharp enough to stay ready for game action.

05.10.10 — SALT LAKE CITY

The story of Game 3 in Utah is the key shot from Derek Fisher at the end of the fourth quarter. The Jazz come up with a great game, especially from the bench and push us right to the limit, 111–110. Here, after Game 4, a fan reaches out from the stands to congratulate Derek as he leaves the floor. He has faced some fan abuse in Utah, where he used to play for the Jazz, so I know he appreciated this gesture.

There it is — the final game in Utah. Pau was terrific! He scored 33 points, and Kobe had 32 in a game we controlled from the first quarter on. Here, he and Kobe congratulate each other over the win. The ability to sweep Utah is key because Phoenix had won its series versus the San Antonio Spurs in short order, sweeping four games. We go on to the conference finals.

05.22.10 — PHOENIX

The players and staff deplane in Phoenix. The series started in Los Angeles with the Lakers showing a dominating inside game, winning the first two games, but now it's our turn to be the visitors. The Suns had the best record in the league after the All-Star break. We are ready for the test, but the Suns have a different idea.

Western Conference Finals: Phoenix

THE SUNS ARE the hottest team in the NBA after the All-Star break. They had a great season with Steve Nash again accelerating the action by his penetrating style of play. Amar'e Stoudemire again is the focus of Nash's drives off screen/roll action, leading the Suns in scoring, but the real change in this team is its bench and its defense. The bench had played a significant role in the Suns' defeat of the San Antonio Spurs in the semifinal round of the Western Conference playoffs. Defensively, they aren't afraid to double-team and rotate, and they are very aggressive.

Again, our size has been a factor against them during the past two seasons, but without Andrew at full strength, we know it will be a challenge. They also get a player back from the injury list — their starting center, Robin Lopez. I am worried about Jason Richardson's play. He has been a big factor in the Suns' surge, shooting a great percentage on his three-point shots and being a central figure on their fast break.

We want Kobe to be really aggressive with him on the offensive end, and he is. He scores 40 points in Game 1 and sets the tone for the series. For Game 2, we go out to a 12-point lead in the second quarter and win by that margin. We shoot 57.7 percent on field goals and 56.2 percent on three-point shots. LO has been a major factor in both our home games, scoring 17 and 19 points, respectively, off the bench. Then it is time to head to Phoenix.

In the second half of Game 2, the Suns have shown a zone defense. We are aware that they will try to play a zone, but in the two home games in Phoenix, their zone is a bother to us. We lose both games in Phoenix by nine points each. Our patience and ability to penetrate their zone is inconsistent: We hold the ball too long, searching for penetrations, and the Suns leave guys open whom they dared to shoot. The 24-second clock is our worst enemy, ultimately. On their offensive end, the Suns get great contributions from their bench and Lopez, who has the game of his career.

Game 5 in Los Angeles, the pressure is on us to get this victory. It is a tight game, even though we control it, and there are only three lead changes, but Phoenix stays with us. Late in the game with a three-point lead and a nearly fully loaded shot clock, Ron Artest takes a three-point shot. He misses, and Phoenix later comes back with the three-point shot to tie the score. With just seconds on the clock, Kobe puts up a desperation shot that Ron catches and puts back in as the buzzer sounds. He goes from goat to hero in less than a minute.

Game 6, back in Phoenix, we control after the first quarter and keep the game in our end, winning by eight points. Kobe is great, and suddenly Ron's offensive game comes alive, and he contributes 25 points, shooting 4 for 7 on three-point shots. We are back in the Finals!

05.22.10 — PHOENIX

The luggage load for equipment manager Rudy Garciduenas increases twofold during the playoffs, as we bring everything but the kitchen sink just in case. Here, Rudy is handling one of the trunks off the truck that contains treatment equipment used in therapy. The temperature in Phoenix is more than 100 degrees at this time of the year, making this a little different from travel in the middle of January.

05.25.10 — PHOENIX

This is the breakfast meeting of the coaching staff. We eat, then go through our scouting
report and the latest newspaper reports. Going clockwise from the left, the coaches are Chuck
Person, Frank Hamblen, myself, Rasheed Hazzard, Jim Cleamons, and Brian Shaw. These are
the guys who bring the reports and ideas about how the Lakers should get the next win.

05.27.10 — LOS ANGELES

Here is Ron Artest's winning shot in the most important game of the Phoenix series, Game 5 ...
Prior to putting back Kobe's last-second heave, Ron had taken an ill-advised shot that gave Phoenix
a chance to make a three-pointer to tie the game. Ron's alert rebound and put-back here give us
the lead in the series, three games to two, leaving the Suns with their backs to the wall.

05.27.10 — LOS ANGELES

The team's reaction to an unbelievable ending to this 103-101 game tells you just how the players feel about their win and their teammate. This was Ron's second basket of the game. He really wanted to contribute to the effort and boy, did he ever. We had a good laugh in the locker room after this game ... a laugh of relief.

05.29.10 — PHOENIX

Here in Game 6, the players are giving each other support. We play a great road game and are in control for most of it, although the Suns make a valiant comeback in the fourth quarter. Ron's scoring, 25 points, is a big factor. He takes the bait of the Suns' zone and makes his three-point shots.

05.29.10 — PHOENIX

The strength of the Lakers against the Suns has been our inside game. Lamar had some great plays during the series even though Game 6 isn't his best on offense. Here, he is playing inside, scoring off an offensive rebound against the Suns' zone defense. Getting a put-back on the offensive end is critical to winning, especially if an opponent plays a zone defense.

05.29.10 — PHOENIX

"I didn't commit the foul, I was just standing there." ... That is what Andrew is saying, in his own words, after an early foul in the second half. It is frustrating, but part of his job is to stay positive and be ready to get back in the action later. The big guys have to take fouls protecting the basket. That is part of their job.

05.29.10 — PHOENIX

Teamwork. ... Guys working together to get a win requires a great amount of teamwork, as much on the defensive end of the court as the offensive. Here, Pau and LO recognize each other's effort after an offensive opportunity in the second half of the game. Considering how many points these two had in the early games, the Suns' strategy is to use a zone defense to keep them from scoring in the last four games.

05.29.10 — PHOENIX

"Good game — good luck." [Left] Players exchange the final handshakes after
the Phoenix series' last game. These two Suns, Steve Nash (talking with Ron)
and Grant Hill (33), have been terrific competitors in this series. [Above] The
players get together after wins and after losses to acknowledge the effort they
have put into a game. Here, after our 111-103 win, we take a moment in our
"circle" before celebrating going back to the NBA Finals for the third year in a row.
Game 6 is one of the closeout games that a coach loves, a defining victory.

05.29.10 — LOS ANGELES

After the Phoenix series, we arrive home. The NBA Finals won't start until June 3 in L.A. We have a much-needed break. Andy's photo catches me taking my luggage to my car in the parking lot. This is the terminal we fly out of in Los Angeles. The second photo is of Kobe's helicopter taking off for Orange County, an hour's drive away. He says this service has made a big difference in his life.

06.03.10 — LOS ANGELES

The defense of the title begins. Players stretch outside the locker room, waiting for the team to gather for their final circle. This is what we've waited for all season — the chance to defend our title.

Reaching the Ring: The Finals

THE 2010 FINALS is a rematch of the two teams from the 2008 Finals. Boston had won that 2008 series in six games. We had played that Finals without Andrew Bynum, and, of course, Ron Artest was added to our team the past year. Boston had their Big Three and, in this year's playoffs, a rising star in Rajon Rondo. They had added a veteran big man in Rasheed Wallace as a free agent, and then made a late-season trade for Nate Robinson.

We trade wins in our home stands. We win the first game, 102-89, at Staples Center. In the second game, won by Boston 103-94, Ray Allen breaks loose for 32 points. He sets a record for most three-pointers made in a Finals game. In the fourth quarter, they outscore us 31-22, which proves to be the margin of victory. Kobe had taken the challenge to play Rondo, but the Celtics' point guard remains a big factor with a triple-double. We go to Boston worried.

The three games played in Boston are stress-filled. We know this was a scenario similar to 2004, when we lost to Detroit in the Finals. Our guys are ready to play whatever role is needed to win a game in Boston and bring the series back to Los Angeles.

We find that game in Game 3, with Derek Fisher playing the role of hero in the final quarter of our 91-84 win. He is our inspiration on that night.

Games 4 and 5 are Boston's as they come back to take the lead in this series and send us back to L.A. down 3-2 with a must-win on our backs. Game 6 is our game from the first quarter. We are up 51-31 at the end of the half and win the game 89-67. Tex Winter often said that our successes rely on one game in in a series that clearly shows a dominating performance. It sets up a Game 7, which the NBA hadn't seen since the 2005 series between the San Antonio Spurs and the Detroit Pistons.

The Celtics end up being without their center, Kendrick Perkins, who injures his knee in Game 6. I am worried that his replacement, Wallace, will be a factor with his scoring ability, both inside and out. Boston comes out strong, takes an early lead and holds it through the half, 40-34. Kobe is having a struggle from the field. Ron Artest helps keep us in the game. The Celtics come out in the second half ready to tack a bigger lead on us. During a span in which the Celtics' lead stretches to as many as 13 points, I call two timeouts (not reluctantly) and try to get us on the right path. We need to get back to our basic triangle offense. We come back to win that third quarter and are down by four points going into the last quarter.

The final quarter we finally get our offense going with a 30-point quarter. Kobe gets to the line, and Pau creates some offense, both scoring and passing the ball. The final nail in the Boston coffin is a pass from Kobe to Ron, who knocks down a three-point shot. Boston valiantly tries to come back, making three three-pointers, but Kobe puts down two free throws and so does Sasha Vujacic in later offensive possessions. Final score: 83-79.

06.03.10 — LOS ANGELES

[Left] Readying for the game, the players re-up their determination for a win. [Above] Kobe in the open floor going in for a a two-handed stuff — nothing too fancy, as he's aware that he has to "manage" an iffy knee. We were able to get to the basket in the first game versus the Celtics. We outscored them 48-30 in the paint in a 102-89 victory. Those points in the lane are a big factor against Boston, as they are a great defensive team.

06.04.10 — LOS ANGELES

Between games in the Finals, practices have to be held at Staples, if possible. I'm getting the players ready to begin our workout with some of our basic lane drills. Usually, one of the coaches on the staff opens practices with our warm-up drills, but since we have limited time, we jump-start our process. After noon, there will be a media session for half an hour and then Boston will take the court in preparation for our game in two days.

06.04.10 — LOS ANGELES

Kobe and I sit on the sidelines and watch the action on the court. Kobe hasn't practiced since the Oklahoma City series. The final part of practice is to play full court and then go through some shooting drills. We have to shorten our practices during the Finals to accommodate the media. This means our video sessions have to be held later or off site.

06.04.10 — LOS ANGELES

Between games, after our practice and media session at Staples, Derek Fisher [right] and Sasha Vujacic [above] are shown at the Salvation Army Red Shield Youth and Community Center reading and interacting with the kids. Shannon Brown and Josh Powell also attend the opening of the Lakers Reading and Learning Center here, along with former Lakers A.C. Green and James Worthy. This is an NBA–Lakers sponsored event, but the players do enjoy and volunteer for these activities.

06.06.10 — LOS ANGELES

Kobe is shown here waiting to get back in Game 2 while encouraging his teammates. But Boston tightens its defense, and the Celtics come back to beat us by nine points, outscoring us by that margin in the fourth quarter. Ray Allen breaks an NBA Finals record with eight three-point shots in this game. Two statistics are notable: It's Boston 36, L.A. 26, for points in the paint. It's Boston 33, L.A. 15, for points beyond the three-point arc. With the next three games on their court, the Celtics are now in the driver's seat.

06.06.10 — LOS ANGELES

Challenging an inside shot by Paul Pierce in Game 2, Andrew Bynum goes up to try to alter or block the shot. Andrew and Pau provide a great safety net for our defenders on the perimeter by patrolling the lane and challenging shooters. Notice the facial expressions on Paul's face — he's trying to bait the refs into calling a foul.

06.07.10 — TEAM PLANE

Frank Hamblen is diagramming Game 2 and preparing a report for Game 3. On our staff, Frank is the coach whose responsibility is Boston. He goes over each play during the game — all eighty-five to ninety times the Celtics have the ball. Frank is going over his notes from the video and transferring them to a report. "Ham" has seen more than forty years of NBA basketball, and he is one of the most respected coaches in the game.

The next morning we have a five-hour plane ride to Boston to begin the three games on the Celtics' court. Pau is reading a novel. He and Derek read the most during flights. Pau has played great the first two games, averaging 24 points. We have been using our basic plan to bring the ball inside and make the Celtics' defense collapse. We just didn't make them pay by making our outside shots in Game 2.

06.07.10 — BOSTON

[Above] Pau steps off the bus in Boston, before a crowd of fans, looking like he slept most of the way on our cross-country flight. During the playoffs the city provides a police escort and security. [Left] Seat partners: I have no idea what we are talking about, but Mitch is emphasizing his point. He sits on the rules committee for our team during league meetings and has just returned from the last meeting with info about what rules might be changing next year.

06.08.10 — BOSTON

Getting prepared before the game. Lamar Odom sits in a hallway where he can find some peace and listens to some inspirational music. The players are overwhelmed by the press when the locker room opens for forty-five minutes to the media. There is just one small room, and sometimes there are twenty, thirty or more press people in the room.

06.08.10 — BOSTON

"This is the game and now is the time" ... Kobe, preparing for Game 3 of the Finals, is seen during the hour-and-a-half process of having therapy, performed here by team trainer Gary Vitti and therapist Judy Seto. The process involves mobilization of ankles, massage, taping of his ankles and his knee, and then activation to prepare himself for the contest.

06.08.10 — BOSTON

It's Game 3, and I'm chiding NBA official Danny Crawford about a disputed call. My best guess is that Danny has been in the Finals refereeing for the last fifteen years — up to this point he's one of the best in the league.

[Near right] The defining play of Game 3 is this shot by Derek Fisher. He receives the ball in the backcourt and goes seventy feet to score over three Celtics. We teach a "direct line" principle — if no one is between you and the basket, go there — and Fish does, making the play to seal the 91–84 victory. [Far right] Back in the locker room after that heroic fourth quarter, Derek has an emotional release. People don't realize how keyed up our players are to win this series, but in the locker room Fish has a moment to let it out. What a game he played! There was a lot of talk about the matchup between Derek and Ray Allen after Game 2, but in this game Fish comes out on top. Ray was 0 for 13 from the field.

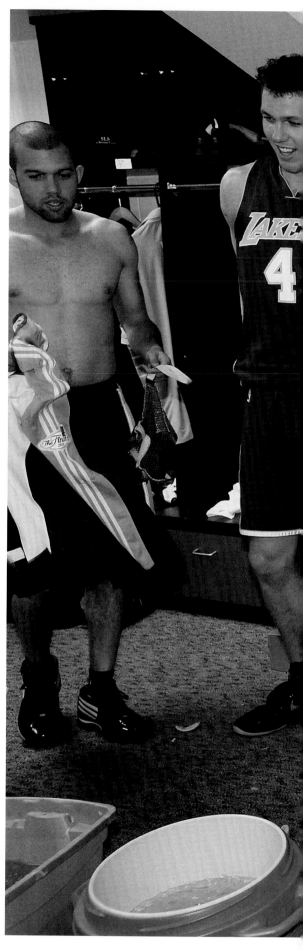

06.08.10 — BOSTON

The coach is at work before the game too: This photo was shot in the locker room while I am filling out the active roster.

06.10.10 — BOSTON

Kobe takes a break from the game to duck into his jersey and wipe the sweat from his face. Many players use their jerseys for a variety of reasons. Sometimes Kobe has his jersey in his mouth, and sometimes I see Sasha with his jersey over his head in frustration or embarrassment. The one I don't like is when a player picks up his jersey and emphasizes his number saying: "It's me." This is a team game.

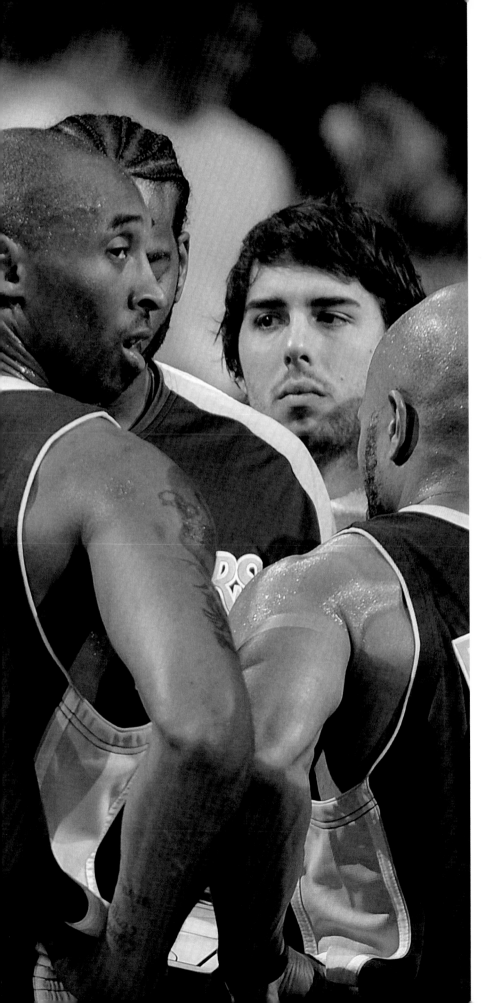

The huddle provides clues to what is going to happen when play begins. Here I'm looking at the situation on the floor or checking the Celtics' huddle to see whether they have a lineup change. Next is to write down the matchups and the situation at hand: Defensively, this relays what Boston likes to do at end-game situations or, on an inbounds play, what we might use to protect — or attempt — a score. Writing with that huge championship ring takes me a couple of playoff games to perfect. I wear the latest ring; I want the players (myself too) to be aware of the reason we're giving our best effort to win. The rings have become very large the last decade.

06.12.10 — BOSTON

The 96-89 loss in Game 4 of the Finals puts us even going into the pivotal Game 5. Here, looking a little tired, Ron is answering questions about the past game. The Boston games start at 9 p.m. on the East Coast, which sets up a very late night. We had the first practice in the morning — with the media at noon. Ron has carried the weight of the team during the playoffs.

06.13.10 — BOSTON

In the hallway in Boston before Game 5, the players get set for warm-ups. Ron is getting the bounce in his legs and Kobe is getting the mind-set he wants before heading out to the floor. As usual, the players are waiting for Sasha to go through his final preparations before the group huddles up for their group act. The cameramen in the hallway now give these private moments the feel of being watched by Big Brother.

06.13.10 — BOSTON

For Game 5, Pau and the team pause for another anthem. We are determined to win this game, but our hopes are dashed by a dogged Boston defense. The inside game of our team has been limited to just 32 points in the lane. Pierce has the best line for the Celtics with 27 points, and Rondo and Garnett each have 18 points to help out.

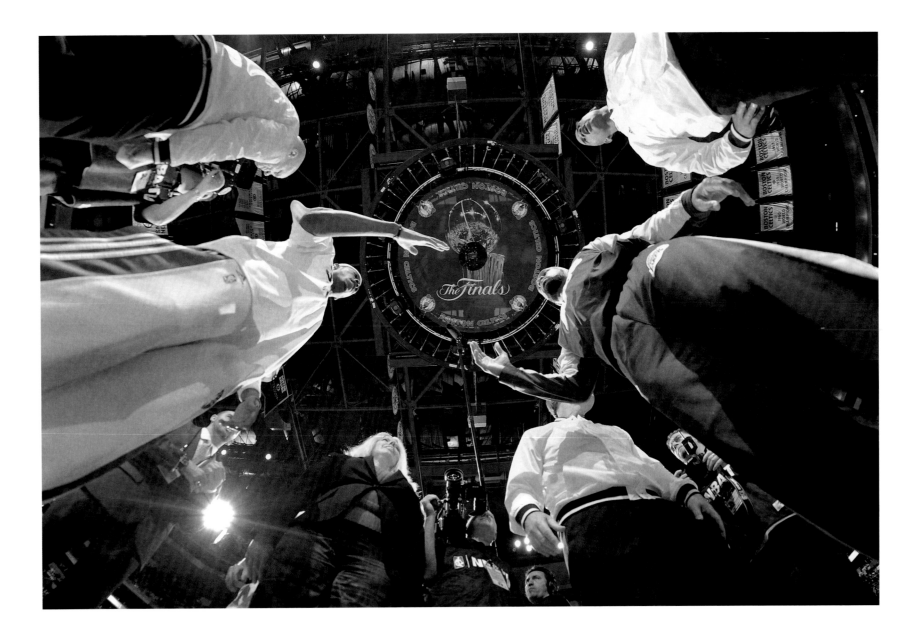

06.13.10 — BOSTON

The fist bump before the game takes place at center circle. Fish and Pierce exchange greetings as the captains meet with the officials to go over the "ground rules" of this game. Once in a while, I'll send a message with our captains to emphasize some feature of the game, i.e. "watch the illegal screen" or something of that ilk.

06.13.10 — BOSTON

Kobe trying to get around Ray Allen and attack the Celtics' defense ... Boston "sat" on Kobe's right hand this series and forced him to go left and then the Celtics came with a big defender to provide "help D." The mark of a great scorer is to be able to beat the defense, even when the opponent sends extra defenders, and either score or find a teammate for an easier shot.

06.13.10 — BOSTON

Kobe has one of those remarkable games, scoring 38 points as he tries to get us back in the game. He has one of the "Bryant"-type runs in the third quarter, but we come up short in a 92-86 loss.

After Game 5, we go back to the locker room and resolve to return to Los Angeles and force a Game 7. Pau carries his bags from a morning flight that brought us into L.A. in midafternoon. We then go right to our facility in El Segundo to get therapy, a short workout and to watch some edited game film in preparation for the game Tuesday.

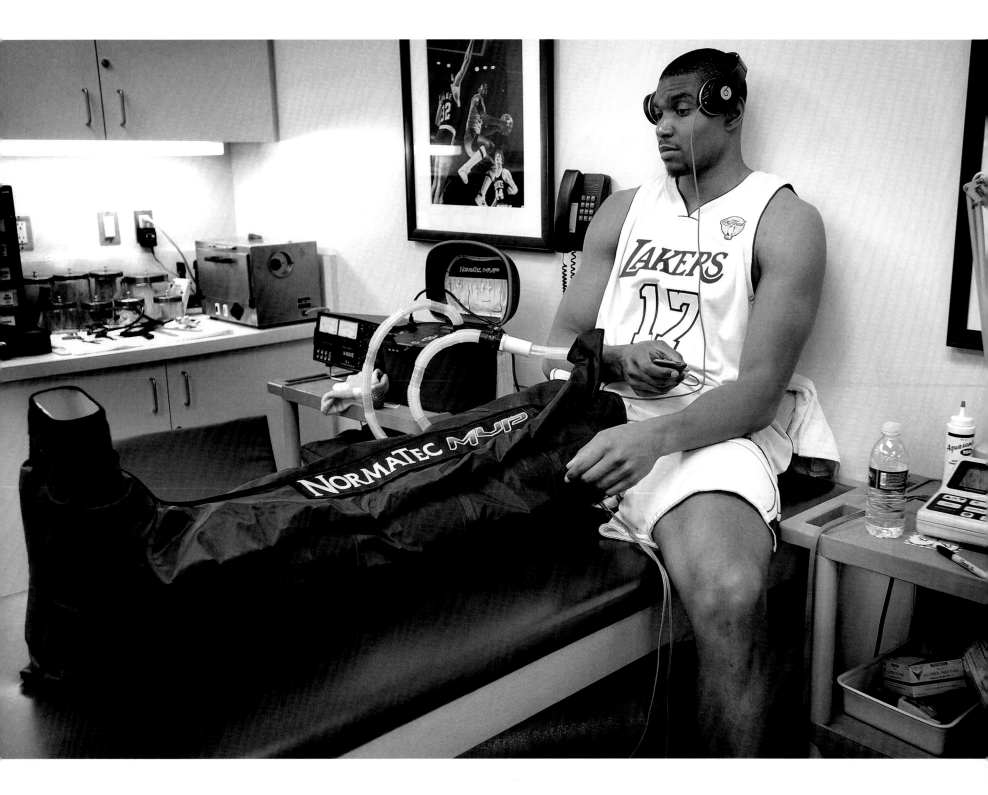

06.15.10 — LOS ANGELES

The daily therapy Bynum has involves this boot that applies pressure and ice-cold temperatures. Here, Drew begins the twenty-minute routine of icing his knee to keep down the swelling while he half-listens to the sounds.

06.15.10 — LOS ANGELES

Making the right play ... After Jordan
draws three defenders who try to prevent
him from scoring, he makes the assist
pass to his teammate for an easy shot.
Notice all five of the Celtics are in the
lane, playing their "help" defense, and
also check out how the Lakers on the
perimeter are "fanning" away from
Jordan, setting themselves up for an
open shot. We build an early lead and
hold on to limit the Celtics to 67 points.

06.15.10 — LOS ANGELES

[Above] Ron, getting advice from the coaching staff in Game 6 ... Ron is the newest member of the Lakers and sometimes needs extra information while on the court. He is more than willing to do the right thing. [Right] The postgame ritual of acknowledging each player catches me congratulating Sasha on his game. The bench was important in this win, redeeming themselves by outscoring the Celtics' bench, 25-13. Sasha hit two big three-pointers, and Jordan made a big hustle play to extend our lead to 51-31 at halftime.

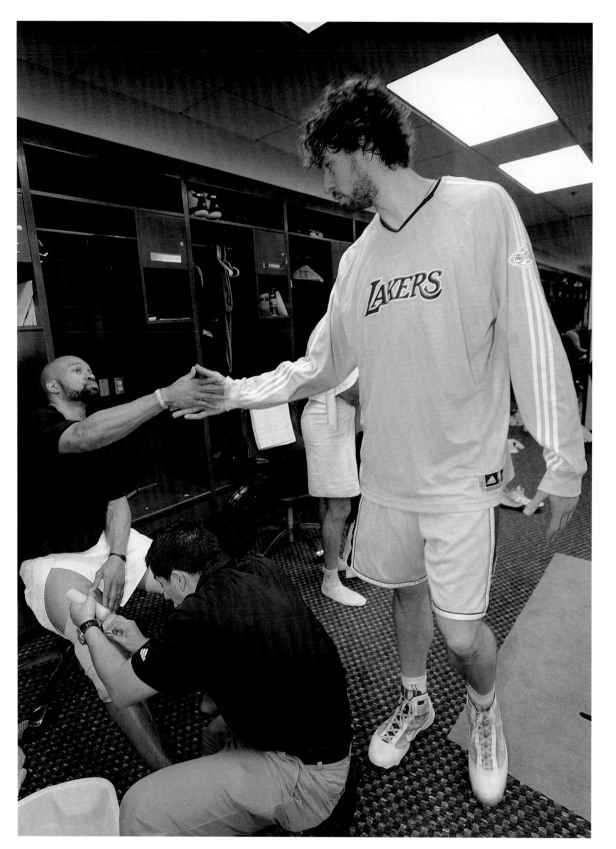

06.15.10 — LOS ANGELES

Derek and Pau give each other some skin in recognition of the work done. Derek had an opportunity to get some much-needed rest, playing only fifteen minutes as our bench gave us a great game. Pau played his normal forty-minute game, scoring 17 points and getting 13 rebounds and 9 assists.

06.15.10 — LOS ANGELES

The postgame ritual involves writing on the board the directions for the next activity of the team. During the playoffs, I write the number of wins left for the championship, a countdown to the ring. This game would allow us to get that coveted title back and win the ring again.

About thirty minutes before the game, we meet in the locker room. During that time, we watch some selected game film and go over our defensive assignments. Before this game it was important for me to address the team about keeping focused on the important ideas and not themselves — to lose themselves in the game. You can see how effective my talk is by the players' rapt attention. In the back of the room you can see one of our therapists, Judy Seto, ready to assist Kobe in his pregame activation. Fish is doing his pregame activation — if you could only see the other side.

06.17.10 — LOS ANGELES

Block or foul? The NBA allows that the hand is part of the ball on this type of shot, and Pau is hopeful that's what the outcome is. Paul Pierce was the Celtics' main guy, and all our players are keyed to help Ron defend him. Ron did a credible job on Pierce as he shot 5 for 15 from the field with 18 points. It was a defensive battle. By now, both teams know what deodorant each other wears, and we have to fight ourselves back into the game after a 34-point first half.

06.17.10 — LOS ANGELES

Locking horns, Paul Pierce and Ron Artest battle under the rim for the right to rebound the ball. This series started with these two going down to the floor fighting for position under the boards. In Game 7, they are still at it — a sign of the competitive nature of both of these players — and neither player backed down.

Pau expresses his emotions, reacting to a play during the game. We come back from a 13-point deficit in the third quarter. Pau is instrumental in the 83-79 win with 19 points, getting a couple of big baskets and feeding Derek Fisher for a three-point shot. Ron was big, scoring 20 points and coming up with a game-clinching three-point shot late in the game. Kobe led the team with 23 hard-earned points.

06.17.10 — LOS ANGELES

The confetti rains on Lamar as he exults in the Lakers' reign. We are so proud of this team's perseverance during the playoffs. It is a great win for these guys, who had to come from behind to beat Boston. They had to battle in three of the four series to pound out the wins. This is the Lakers' 16th championship and the 10th title for the franchise under Dr. Buss' ownership.

06.17.10 — LOS ANGELES

Shannon Brown passing the trophy around the team, while Ron is hugging Kobe ... All the players and all of our staff and some of the owner's family — and someone else's family member, Miss Natalia Bryant — were on the podium after the trophy presentation by Commissioner David Stern. This is the moment that all players want to experience. We are one joyful team.

06.17.10 — LOS ANGELES

"Thanks go to you — the Lakers' 'sixth man.'" ... My turn at the podium after the seventh game, and here I am thanking the Lakers fans for their heartfelt support. We needed home-court advantage to win this series. The walk from the court to the locker room is filled with well-wishers. I'm usually one to acknowledge the fans with only a wave or a smile, but here I'm giving somebody a high-five.

06.17.10 — LOS ANGELES

This photo is taken in the coaches' locker room. I'm hanging up my suit coat, getting ready to go get my champagne shower. There is nothing like a championship locker room filled with noise and celebration. I actually have champagne shoes to wear for this mess, but they have been retired for the past two championships.

06.17.10 — LOS ANGELES

The Caps with their caps getting their shower and celebrating in their own way ... [Above] Team captain Kobe is taking it all in, while team captain Fish [left] has both the Wheaties box with our team photo proclaiming "Back to Back NBA Champions" and the trophy in his hands. The locker room is draped with plastic covering and even the cameramen are covered up. We are all aglow. These two guys have really collaborated this season to keep the team moving forward toward this goal.

06.17.10 — LOS ANGELES

"Will the circle be unbroken"
… This is our final meeting in
a circle to have the last words
and to feast on the joy of our
union. My champagne shower.
Our normal shout has been:
"1-2-3 Ring!" After this year's
victory, that phrase will take
on even more meaning while
we try to do the remarkable
X3 ["Times Three"] journey
toward another championship.

06.17.10 — LOS ANGELES

As I towel off after the bath, Kobe comes over to share his feeling about that game. After the win, he has often said that his teammates bailed him out, as he was so determined to win the game and had such a tough night shooting the ball. It is a remarkable feat: He has now moved into an elite circle in the NBA.

06.17.10 — LOS ANGELES

Kobe expresses the joy he feels at winning his fifth title. This was by far the most difficult of his career. He had to nurse a bum knee for the last three playoff rounds and played even better under that discomfort. I know this one means a lot to him because it gives him one more than his buddy, Shaq.

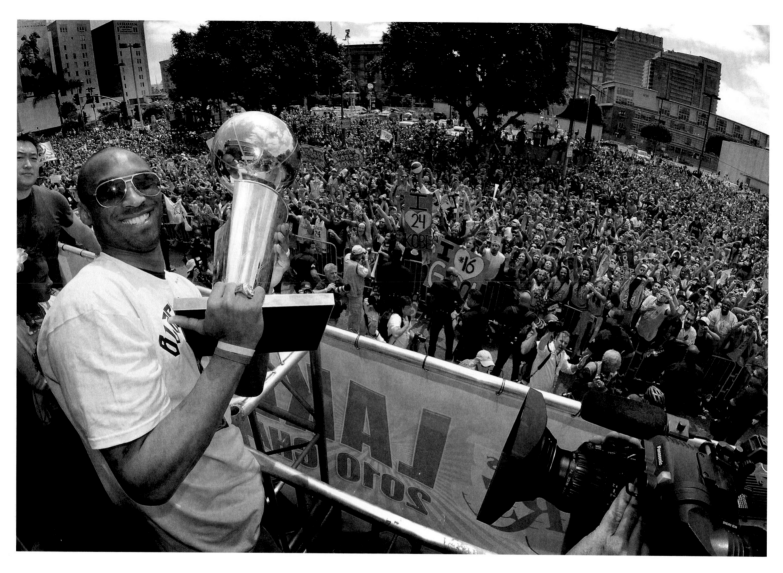

06.21.10 — LOS ANGELES

The parade of champions ... [Above] Kobe holds the trophy before a group of
fans while the cameras whir. [Right] Pau gives his blessing to the Lakers' faithful
as the bus goes by St. Vincent's Catholic Church on Figueroa Street. There was
a crowd of more than 50,000 fans who celebrated with the players as they
went through downtown Los Angeles. A lot of these fans don't get a chance
to get into the games, and it's great to celebrate the victory with them.

CAST OF CHARACTERS

RON ARTEST

Queensbridge, NY • Joined team in 2009

SHANNON BROWN

Maywood, IL • Joined team in 2009

KOBE BRYANT

Philadelphia, PA • Joined team in 1996

ANDREW BYNUM

Plainsboro, NJ • Joined team in 2005

JORDAN FARMAR

Los Angeles, CA • Joined team in 2006

DEREK FISHER

Little Rock, AR • Joined team in 1996 (–2004); rejoined in 2007

PAU GASOL

Sant Boi de Llobrega, Spain • Joined team in 2008

DJ MBENGA

Kinshasa, Congo • Joined team in 2008

ADAM MORRISON

Glendive, MT • Joined team in 2009

LAMAR ODOM

Jamaica, NY • Joined team in 2004

JOSH POWELL

Charleston, SC • Joined team in 2008

SASHA VUJACIC

Maribor, Slovenia • Joined team in 2004

LUKE WALTON

San Diego, CA • Joined team in 2003

PHIL JACKSON
Deer Lodge, MT • Joined team in 1999 (–2004); rejoined in 2005

Acknowledgments

AUGUST 2010 — The process of going through Andy's photographs of the last season was a special pleasure because it brought back so many good memories, so my thanks to Andy Bernstein. The past season wasn't an easy year, as we had to endure a lot of road trips in the last half of the season, but thanks to my support staff for making it as good as it could be. Narda Zacchino, thanks for your editing and patience over our Internet relationship.

Of course, my thanks to Jeanie Buss, my sweetheart, who talked me into the Second Coming with the Lakers. My assistant, Gayle Waller, who keeps my life on an even keel, and Linda Rambis for encouraging me to do the book, thanks.

I just couldn't have done this work without the thirteen players on the team. They keep my life very interesting, to say the least. To my group of writer friends who continue to encourage me to express myself by writing, thanks for the pats on the back. Thanks also to the Lakers' management for their patience with my quips and quotes that hover on the razor's edge, even though some may result in penalties. To my teacher, Roshi Kwong, who encourages me to step on that edge and experience life in all its many forms, KiKi-SoSo.

—*Phil Jackson*

AUGUST, 2010 — I am appreciative to many at the Lakers organization for welcoming me as part of the team so I could accomplish this project. First and foremost I want to thank Phil Jackson for his trust and support throughout. I would also like to thank Jeanie Buss, Tim Harris, Mitch Kupchak, Tania Jolly, Kristen Luken, John Black, Alison Bogli, Josh Rupprecht, Linda Rambis, Gayle Waller, Eugenia Chow, Gary Vitti, and Rudy Garciduenas for their help. Also thanks to Rob Pelinka of Landmark Sports Agency for his assistance.

From the NBA I would like to thank David Stern, Adam Silver, Joel Litvin, David Denenberg, Charlie Rosenzweig, John Hareas, Joe Amati, Dion Cocoros, and Andy Thompson. I would also like to thank my crew in Los Angeles for their hard work and for putting up with some of my unusual ideas: Noah Graham, Evan Gole, Johnny Vy, Juan Ocampo, and Wendi Kaminski.

Thanks also to Lee Zeidman, Michael Roth, and Cara Vanderhook of AEG and Staples Center; and Carmin Romanelli and Mike Klein of Getty Images. Special thanks to Kelly Ryan and Sean McFarland for their friendship, guidance, and support.

This book would not exist without the hard-working crew at Time Capsule Press: Narda Zacchino, Dickson Louie, Tom Trapnell, Mike Zacchino, Karen Chaderjian, and Hans Tesselaar. Thank you all.

Very special thanks to all of my wonderful family, especially my wife Mariel Mulet, and children, Michael, Helena, Juliet, and Emilia. Thank you for your understanding, patience, and love.

—*Andrew D. Bernstein*

Afterword

BY ANDREW D. BERNSTEIN

Phil Jackson has been an integral figure in my professional life for more than twenty years. We have spent many a June together, with his winning eleven NBA titles — from his first with the Chicago Bulls in 1991 through his most recent with the Lakers in 2010 — and my recording them with my camera.

In the summer of 2009, after Phil's Lakers had won the NBA championship, I had been thinking of a way to approach the upcoming season differently from my previous twenty-seven years. I understood Phil's philosophy of an NBA season being a nine-month journey, and I decided to document this one in black and white photography from training camp to the end of the road — hopefully a championship victory parade.

With Phil's approval and the help of the Lakers' public relations staff headed by John Black, the project took shape as training camp opened at the end of September 2009. I was granted behind-the-scenes access to the inner sanctum of the Lakers — practices, plane flights, locker room meetings, and training room preparations. Over many years I have established a great comfort level with the players and staff, knowing how to get my photos and not infringe on the team's private time and space.

Most of these photos were shot in black and white, which lent itself to the documentary feel I wanted to portray. Some were converted from the original color to keep the look consistent. The professional digital cameras I use allow for a quick switch from color to black and white. The player portraits were shot originally on medium format film that I believe brought out a richness and depth. The four-color printing process further enhances the overall quality of the book.

Many of these photos were moments I captured through careful technical preparation honed by years of experience, such as utilizing remote cameras set up hours before the game in the catwalk and strategic areas of the arena, above the shot clock, behind the backboard, or buried within the base of the basket support. Each regular-season game calls for a setup of a minimum of ten cameras, which ramps up to more than twenty for the playoffs and Finals.

In this book, Phil and I recount quite a journey in 2009-10; we hope you enjoyed coming along for the ride.

Index

Lakers 2009-10 Schedule | Game by Game

Regular-Season Schedule

DATE	OPPONENT	W-L	SCORE
10/27/09	LA Clippers	1-0	W 99-92
10/30/09	Dallas	1-1	L 80-94
11/01/09	Atlanta	2-1	W 118-110
11/03/09	@Oklahoma City	3-1	W 101-98 OT
11/04/09	@ Houston	4-1	W 103-102 OT
11/06/09	Memphis	5-1	W 111-98
11/08/09	New Orleans	6-1	W 104-98
11/12/09	Phoenix	7-1	W 121-102
11/13/09	@ Denver	7-2	L 79-105
11/15/09	Houston	7-3	L 91-101
11/17/09	Detroit	8-3	W 106-93
11/19/09	Chicago	9-3	W 108-93
11/22/09	Oklahoma City	10-3	W 101-85
11/24/09	NY Knicks	11-3	W 100-90
11/28/09	@ Golden State	12-3	W 130-97
11/29/09	New Jersey	13-3	W 106-87
12/01/09	New Orleans	14-3	W 110-99
12/04/09	Miami	15-3	W 108-107
12/06/09	Phoenix	16-3	W 108-88
12/09/09	Utah	17-3	W 101-77
12/11/09	Minnesota	18-3	W 104-92
12/12/09	@ Utah	18-4	L 94-102
12/15/09	@ Chicago	19-4	W 96-87
12/16/09	@ Milwaukee	20-4	W 107-106 OT
12/19/09	@ New Jersey	21-4	W 103-83
12/20/09	@ Detroit	22-4	W 93-81
12/22/09	Oklahoma City	23-4	W 111-108
12/25/09	Cleveland	23-5	L 87-102
12/26/09	@ Sacramento	24-5	W 112-103 OT
12/28/09	@ Phoenix	24-6	L 103-118
12/29/09	Golden State	25-6	W 124-118
01/01/10	Sacramento	26-6	W 109-108
01/03/10	Dallas	27-6	W 131-96
01/05/10	Houston	28-6	W 88-79
01/06/10	@ LA Clippers	28-7	L 91-102
01/08/10	@ Portland	28-8	L 98-107
01/10/10	Milwaukee	29-8	W 95-77
01/12/10	@ San Antonio	29-9	L 85-105
01/13/10	@ Dallas	30-9	W 100-95
01/15/10	LA Clippers	31-9	W 126-86
01/18/10	Orlando	32-9	W 100-95
01/21/10	@ Cleveland	32-10	L 87-93
01/22/10	@ NY Knicks	33-10	W 115-105
01/24/10	@ Toronto	33-11	L 105-106
01/26/10	@ Washington	34-11	W 115-103
01/27/10	@ Indiana	35-11	W 118-96
01/29/10	@ Philadelphia	36-11	W 99-91
01/31/10	@ Boston	37-11	W 90-89
02/01/10	@ Memphis	37-12	L 93-95
02/03/10	Charlotte	38-12	W 99-97
02/05/10	Denver	38-13	L 113-126
02/06/10	@ Portland	39-13	W 99-82
02/08/10	San Antonio	40-13	W 101-89
02/10/10	@ Utah	41-13	W 96-81
02/16/10	Golden State	42-13	W 104-94
02/18/10	Boston	42-14	L 86-87
02/23/10	@ Memphis	43-14	W 99-98
02/24/10	@ Dallas	43-15	L 96-101
02/26/10	Philadelphia	44-15	W 99-90
02/28/10	Denver	45-15	W 95-89
03/02/10	Indiana	46-15	W 122-99
03/04/10	@ Miami	46-16	L 111-114 OT
03/05/10	@ Charlotte	46-17	L 83-98
03/07/10	@ Orlando	46-18	L 94-96
03/09/10	Toronto	47-18	W 109-107
03/12/10	@ Phoenix	48-18	W 102-96
03/15/10	@ Golden State	49-18	W 124-121
03/16/10	@ Sacramento	50-18	W 106 - 99
03/19/10	Minnesota	51-18	W 104-96
03/21/10	Washington	52-18	W 99-92
03/24/10	@ San Antonio	53-18	W 99-92
03/26/10	@ Oklahoma City	53-19	L 75-91
03/27/10	@ Houston	54-19	W 109-101
03/29/10	@ New Orleans	54-20	L 100-108
03/31/10	@ Atlanta	54-21	L 92-109
04/02/10	Utah	55-21	W 106-92
04/04/10	San Antonio	55-22	L 81-100
04/08/10	@ Denver	55-23	L 96-98
04/09/10	@ Minnesota	56-23	W 97-88
04/11/10	Portland	56-24	L 88-91
04/13/10	Sacramento	57-24	W 106-100
04/14/10	@ LA Clippers	57-25	L 91-107

NBA Playoffs, First Round

DATE	OPPONENT	W-L	SCORE
04/18/10	Oklahoma City	1-0	W 87-79
04/20/10	Oklahoma City	2-0	W 95-92
04/22/10	@ Oklahoma City	2-1	L 96-101
04/24/10	@ Oklahoma City	2-2	L 89-110
04/27/10	Oklahoma City	3-2	W 111-87
04/30/10	@ Oklahoma City	4-2	W 95-94

Western Conference Semifinals

DATE	OPPONENT	W-L	SCORE
05/02/10	Utah	1-0	W 104-99
05/04/10	Utah	2-0	W 111-103
05/08/10	@Utah	3-0	W 111-110
05/10/10	@ Utah	4-0	W 111-96

Western Conference Finals

DATE	OPPONENT	W-L	SCORE
05/17/10	Phoenix	1-0	W 128-107
05/19/10	Phoenix	2-0	W 124-112
05/23/10	@ Phoenix	2-1	L 109-118
05/25/10	@ Phoenix	2-2	L 106-115
05/27/10	Phoenix	3-2	W 103-101
05/29/10	@ Phoenix	4-2	W 111-103

NBA Finals

DATE	OPPONENT	W-L	SCORE
06/03/10	Boston	1-0	W 102-89
06/06/10	Boston	1-1	L 94-103
06/08/10	@ Boston	2-1	W 91-84
06/10/10	@ Boston	2-2	L 89-96
06/13/10	@ Boston	2-3	L 86-92
06/15/10	Boston	3-3	W 89-67
06/17/10	Boston	4-3	W 83-79